TEACHING WRITING ONLINE

Teaching Writing Online
How and Why

Scott Warnock
Drexel University

National Council of Teachers of English
1111 W. Kenyon Road, Urbana, Illinois 61801-1096

Copy Editor: JAS Group
Production Editor: Carol Roehm-Stogsdill
Interior Design: Jenny Jensen Greenleaf
Cover Design: Pat Mayer
Cover Image: iStockphoto.com/Andrey Prokhorov

NCTE Stock Number: 52539

It is the policy of NCTE in its journals and other publications to provide a forum for the open discussion of ideas concerning the content and the teaching of English and the language arts. Publicity accorded to any particular point of view does not imply endorsement by the Executive Committee, the Board of Directors, or the membership at large, except in announcements of policy, where such endorsement is clearly specified.

Every effort has been made to provide current URLs and email addresses, but because of the rapidly changing nature of the Web, some sites and addresses may no longer be accessible.

Library of Congress Cataloging-in-Publication Data

Warnock, Scott, 1967–
    Teaching writing online : how and why / Scott Warnock.
       p. cm.
    Includes bibliographical references and index.
    ISBN 978-0-8141-5253-9 (pbk.)
    1. English language—Rhetoric—Study and teaching (Higher)—Computer-assisted instruction. 2. College students—Effect of technological innovations on. 3. Language and the Internet. I. Title.
    PE1404.W37 2009
    808'.0420785—dc22

                                  2009014662

To Julianne, who helps me through.

CONTENTS

CONTENTS

INTRODUCTION

Migrating *to Online Writing Instruction:*
How, Why, and Who

The philosophy that underlies my approach to teaching writing online is that you can migrate *your teaching style and strategies to the online environment. I describe that philosophy below while explaining the structure of this book to you, my reader.*

My objective is to share my experiences as an online writing teacher and faculty trainer to help other teachers teach composition effectively with digital tools. Along the way, I will also explain how teaching online opens an array of intriguing teaching and learning opportunities for writing instructors and their students.

I joined Drexel University in the summer of 2004. One of the primary reasons I was hired was to guide a new initiative in the Department of English and Philosophy to offer first-year writing (**FYW**) courses in fully online formats. I became the leader of a group called the Online Writing Teachers (OWT); we worked throughout the summer of 2004 to prepare online versions of our first-year writing courses, starting with English 101: Expository Writing and Reading. (I describe the roller coaster–like experiences of that initial summer in the article "And Then There Were Two: The Growing Pains of an Online Writing Course Faculty Training Initiative.") As OWT team leader, I have worked during the past few years with teachers who have a wide variety of experience with and interest in learning technologies. As I have refined my own approaches to teaching online and **hybrid courses,**

I have developed faculty training workshops, created faculty development materials, and devoted hundreds of hours to one-on-one sessions with teachers who were learning how to incorporate teaching technologies into their pedagogical approaches. All of these activities have worked synergistically with my research and scholarly interests, which increasingly have focused on issues involved in using learning technologies to teach writing. In training and working with so many teachers, I began to realize that although resources for teaching online are plentiful, materials specifically designed for teaching writing online and the teaching philosophy that accompanies online composition instruction are scarce. It was with that realization that I decided to write this book.

I have found online writing instruction promising and intriguing for many reasons. **OWcourses** (bolded terms are defined in the glossary) offer opportunities to teach beyond the normal constraints of geographic and temporal borders. Indeed, students of all kinds continue to swell the enrollments in online classes. The Sloan-C report *Staying the Course: Online Education in the United States, 2008* indicates that the growth rate of online enrollments was 12.9 percent, compared with 1.2 percent overall U.S. growth in higher education enrollments, and more than 20 percent of U.S. students took an online course in fall 2007 (Allen and Seaman 1), so it appears that opportunities to expand our instructional offerings with online methods will continue to increase. The International Society for Technology in Education (ISTE) issued revised technology standards for teachers in June 2008, and the creators "began with the assumption this time that every teacher recognizes the importance of technology and how it can transform teaching and learning," said Lajeane Thomas, chair of ISTE's standards committee and director of the group's National Educational Technology Standards project ("ISTE Unveils," par. 5). Technology is increasingly becoming a given in instructional design—the question now is not *if*, but *how* teachers will use it.

Online instruction itself opens a number of opportunities, but I specifically find online *writing* instruction promising because I believe—and this is a core premise of this book—that online writing instruction provides the opportunity for not just a *different* approach, but a *progressive* approach to the way teachers teach writing—an evolution of sorts in writing instruction. This belief stems from several factors inherent in the OWcourse. One is the sheer amount of writing exchanged among students and the teacher in an OWcourse; few onsite courses offer the chance for this amount of writing. Second is the number of opportunities that open up when students create so much writing, much of it informal and developmental. The third factor is that because the interactions in OWcourse format that I describe in this book are almost entirely written, students are faced with a unique educational challenge/pressure to write to communicate almost everything in the course.

"Teaching online privileges writing in ways that traditional classes cannot," wrote Susanmarie Harrington, Rebecca Rickly, and Michael Day in the introduction to their book, *The Online Writing Classroom*, because so much of the communication in an online class is through writing (8). Thomas Barker and Fred Kemp have called this ongoing reading and writing practice "*textualizing* the class" (20). Juan Flores prefers teaching FYW online because these "almost entirely text-based . . . environments require from students a constant and independently active participation in their own learning. Students not only learn to think through their reading and writing . . . but to engage in reflective thinking over the writing of others" (430). When you migrate your writing course online, students are writing to you and to each other in virtually all of their course communications, expanding ideas of audience, purpose, and context each time they contribute to a message board, create a **blog** entry, or engage in an email-based peer review. In that way, I see the possibilities of a progressive step toward, perhaps, a "better" composition class, and I expand on this premise throughout the book. Why *better*? Because the online format—*by its very nature*—requires students to learn to use writing to interact with others. Many teachers have reproduced this experience in onsite courses, but in the OWcourse, students often have little fallback position: if they want to express something in the course, they must write it. The OWcourse forces an environment that is not just writing intensive but also often writing exclusive. As writing teachers, we couldn't ask for a better lab or workshop to help our first-year students develop their ability to communicate using the written word.

Indeed, OWcourses allow teachers to enact many theoretical, and sometimes otherwise logistically tricky, ideas about composition pedagogy. The ideas of many compositional thinkers who strongly influenced my teaching practices are enlivened and, in some cases, given full form for perhaps the first time in the online learning environment. James Britton and his coauthors, for instance, recognized decades ago that children learn to write largely by writing (3). Kenneth Bruffee's ideas about collaborative learning, Linda Flower and John Hayes's ideas about composing, Peter Elbow's ideas about invention and risk, the **WAC** (writing across the curriculum) school's mantra of writing to learn—these concepts find new expression in the OWcourse environment. Julie Wood pointed out the natural link between computers and process-centered writing pedagogy, saying of the computer that students "learn to use this highly-flexible tool in ways that help them develop as writers in the truest sense" (par. 3). She expanded on the ideas of Edward Fiske, who observed the synergy for children between the writing process approach and the use of technology when he noted, "Computers are the most important new technology for writing instruction since the invention of the pencil—maybe even more so. Learning to write is essentially self-editing. . . . For little children, the biggest obstacle to learning to write is the physical act of moving the pencil across the paper, but computers make this unnecessary" (157). Some reasons for the natural connections between computers and composition have to do with theoretical ideas about digital writing; but others are straightforward, because the online environment enables the easy dissemination, sharing, and revising of texts. The continuous writing environment makes it ever possible for students to learn through their own work in a studio-like environment (Grego and Thompson 8). Computers and composition specialists have long been intrigued by the collaborative writing and knowledge potential of the *hivemind*, as Don Byrd and Derek Owens called it, where the informational hive exists only "as the contact among people who realize a shared consciousness within the sustained event of that writing" (55). These ideas come to the fore in the OWcourse.

Throughout this book, I offer a series of core guidelines to help direct you in the most important things you might consider as you prepare to teach online. Here is the first:

Guideline 1: Teaching writing online offers you new ways to apply theoretical and pedagogical concepts about writing. It can provide you with different ways of disseminating, sharing, reviewing, and responding to student texts.

Some go so far as to say that in many composition classrooms, writing is "taught only incidentally" (Kitzhaber 36), but I will simply state here that the OWcourse allows us to refocus our teaching efforts on the core element of the FYW course: written work our students create.

Migration: A Concept That Can Work for New Online Teachers

This book operates from a premise that contradicts what many experts in online instruction have said about the transition to the electronic teaching environment. Many say that online teaching is completely different from onsite or face-to-face (**f2f**) teaching. In an effort to emphasize the potential of the online environment, these experts often highlight acute differences between online and onsite teaching. For instance, right up front in *Conquering the Content*, Robin Smith stated that online learning "is very different" from classroom learning, so onsite teaching materials that worked before are "not going to be suitable for Web-based teaching," and the resulting adjustment is "tough" for faculty (4–5). In their book *Teaching Online*, Susan Ko and Steve Rossen were more reserved but still contended that "a strict translation of what you normally do on the ground into the online environment isn't always desirable" (45). Although I understand that we want to prevent teachers from moving online casually, I think that these types of cautions plunge new teachers immediately into a zone of uncertainty, where they may feel there is too much to overcome to begin teaching online.

I believe that you can approach teaching online more confidently if you view it as *not* being that different from teaching onsite. I say this not just because I think that people who perceive online instruction as totally alien to their normal, tried-and-true teaching practices are often scared off from teaching online, but because teaching online, like teaching onsite, is about recognizing your teaching talent zones or areas and finding ways to translate those talents to the teaching environment in which you are working. Barbara Stedman states this well: "Know your pedagogy, find those points where pedagogy and technology genuinely meet, and develop highly specific goals, tasks, and instructions that facilitate such a union" (28). This book investigates the many good ways to make this transition, and I believe that if you focus on what you do well in the classroom, you will find the move to online teaching less difficult—and more enjoyable.

Even authors who caution about the stark difference between online and onsite teaching do recognize that core strategies can be preserved. For instance, despite the initial warnings above, Smith also pointed out that central teaching concepts, such as Arthur Chickering and Zelda Gamson's seven principles for undergraduate teaching, still apply regardless of modality: contact between students and faculty, reciprocity and cooperation among students, active learning, time on task, feedback, communicating high expectations, and respecting diverse talents and ways of learning (6). Ko and Rossen, too, could see how "converting your course to an online environment means adapting it to use some of the tools available in the new environment" (36). And Patricia Addesso said that contrary to what many think, "there are many transferable skills between traditional and online facilitation" (113). Like these authors, I recognize that teaching online is different from teaching onsite, perhaps as different as teaching a writing course in two radically different parts of the world, but the foundation of what you do *conceptually* can still remain very much the same. Remember that you don't have to "dazzle students to be effective" (Ko and Rossen 40) in online instruction. In short, I have become convinced that good onsite teachers who are willing to spend some time developing their technological literacy can quickly become good online teachers.

Actually, the reason that some teachers may be scared of moving to a fully online environment is that they need to do something that, as a teacher, can be painful and even a wee bit embarrassing: closely evaluate your own teaching. As we all know, we often find it difficult to determine whether the things we do in the writing classroom are effective. We *think* and often *hope* they are effective, but the reality is that we often simply do not know. (In 2000, Richard Haswell said that the 40-year-old mission of documenting how college students change their writing "has not been much advanced by researchers" ["Documenting" 307].) I think that most dedicated teachers—writing or otherwise, including people in any profession of which teaching/mentoring is a foundation—go through periodic moments of malaise during which they suspect that everything they are doing is wrong; they may even wonder if they are doing things exactly *opposite* to the way they should be done. That's an unsettling feeling, and I have gone through similar cycles during my decade and a half of teaching. Part of the problem that some teachers have when migrating to online teaching is that malaise and uncertainty seem to bubble up from their very classroom souls—while they are trying to learn a new *course management system* (**CMS**). (I prefer the term *learning management system* [LMS], but generally LMS is used for corporate training incarnations of e-learning, whereas CMS is used for learning on the academic side.) The combination of these constraints can be enough to make some teachers want to give up. I hope to help you feel comfortable about converting what you do in the onsite classroom, so that this teaching introspection can lead to discoveries, not frustrations, and help you see technology as a productive partner in this development of your teaching abilities.

The *How*: Writing Instruction Is Different

One focus of this book is on the *How*. How do you teach writing in an online environment? I want you, the teacher, to use this book as a guide to help you take instructional strategies that have worked in the onsite classroom and migrate them to the online environment. Many teachers can become rapidly acclimated to the online environment if they think about migrating their long-developed skills, instead of thinking an OWcourse requires a brand-new teaching approach. So let's consider what this means (which may also help you choose the chapters in this book most applicable to you). Say that your class . . .

◆ **is built around conversations your students have about readings.** You will want to think about how your moderator skills transfer to the e-environment, facilitating message boards, listservs, chats, and other conversational technologies. (See Chapters 7 and 8.)

◆ **is built around highly student-centered conversations.** You can use a variety of online communication tools to de-emphasize your role in conversations. In fact, students can take over the conversation in an online environment perhaps even more effectively than they can with you present in the f2f room. (See Chapter 8.)

◆ **uses lots of workshop-like peer evaluations of student writing.** You can use similar strategies in perhaps even more efficient and effective ways online. (See Chapter 10.)

◆ **relies on content lessons about the course subject matter.** There are numerous ways to convert such materials. Content delivery is the common paradigm for many guides to online instruction. (See Chapter 4.)

◆ **is based on personalized interaction you have with your students about their formal writing projects.** You can use many different strategies to provide comments on students' writing. If you have always provided comments in handwriting, you will find new opportunities for individual feedback and broader assessment in online instruction. (See Chapter 11.)

◆ **involves quizzing.** Almost any CMS provides quizzes. (See Chapters 7 and 12.)

◆ **involves presentations.** Most software tools allow you to facilitate student presentations. Voice tools are continually improving; and using other technology tools, you can achieve multimedia capability with assignments and presentations. (See Chapters 3 and 14.)

◆ **features your efforts to model writing.** With audiovisual (AV) technologies, you can provide highly stimulating lessons that feature you as the writer. Using these technologies, students can also revisit these lessons. (See Chapter 3.)

> **Guideline 2**: Initially, you want to think *migration*, not *transformation*, when teaching online. Think about what you do well, and then think about how you can use various resources to *translate* those skills to the OWcourse.

Although I cover many general aspects of teaching online in the following chapters, I want you to understand that the technical instructions for almost all online tools are covered well elsewhere, as are instructions for teaching online in general. There are many fine websites, articles, and books on the topic of teaching online, and I list some particularly useful resources in Chapter 18. (In terms of technical instruction, the best source for this kind of information may be your own campus's IT department.) This book focuses on the specifics of teaching *writing* courses online. I will try to help you understand how to bring together some of the basic tools and strategies of the writing teacher's trade using online tools and techniques: How do I conduct a peer review? What constitutes a useful **informal writing** assignment? What's the best way to provide feedback on student papers? The chapters address the main areas teachers need to understand to teach writing effectively online.

One thing is certain: you want to "consider your course objectives, the preferred teaching strategies and approaches to the material that you want to preserve, and any new approaches you would like to try in the online environment." In terms of course design, you want to make sure "course objectives are defined in terms of the **learning outcomes**" and that all activities in your course are aligned with those outcomes as well (Ko and Rossen 46). In this way, you will be engaging in the same kind of internal Socratic dialogue as in preparing for any teaching experience: asking yourself questions about how you want to teach the course and what you hope students will take from that learning experience.

A Certain Style of Teaching

Note that I emphasize a certain style of online teaching in this book. I will mention other approaches, but my core approach to teaching online involves the intensive use of **asynchronous** writing tools in an already packaged CMS. *Asynchronous* means using technology tools that do not require all students to be present at the same time; so your students write when they wish, as opposed to attending a class electronically at a specific time and using chat or voice software to participate in real time.

There are many tools you could use to teach online, but because I assume you are new to online instruction, I think the best way for you to progress is to use an already available CMS, probably provided and supported at some level by your institution. Some object to the use of a password-protected CMS in an era of open-source information, but I think your writing students need to operate in a semiprivate, safe area of the Web, and your institution's CMS accomplishes that. You can also teach online by using voice technologies and convening the class electronically, or by using a combination of external blog, **wiki**, and message board software. I will mention many of these options, but I will focus on a certain method that I think can be used effectively by most teachers. If you become interested in this mode of teaching, you will soon discover that in terms of technology, the possibilities are endless; but I'll assume that you want to lower the technology barrier as much as you can, and for teachers new to the online environment, that means using a prepackaged CMS.

Guideline 3: Most prepackaged course management systems (CMS) have everything you need to help you translate your pedagogy to the OWcourse.

The *Why* of Teaching Writing Online

As Nietsche once said, in a more dramatic context, "If you have your *why?* for life, then you can get along with almost any *how?*" (6).

I don't want you to "bear" the responsibility of online instruction carelessly or blindly, but in explaining how to teach writing online, I also express what I consider important reasons for us to explore this teaching modality. One of the primary reasons is that this environment, as I mentioned, can be purely textual. Students are in a rich, guided learning environment in which they express themselves to a varied audience with their written words. Even if you are reluctant to teach hybrid or online courses, the electronic communication tools in every CMS allow your students to write to you and to each other in ways that will open up teaching and learning opportunities for everyone involved.

OWcourses can also be more than just textual environments for students. They can provide a needed method of delivering courses to people whose lives have undergone significant disruption. After Hurricane Katrina in 2005, I not only used electronic tools to volunteer teach a Sloan-C-sponsored composition course, but I also was able to place the New Orleans student who enrolled in the course—the only student who was able to make the whole process work well enough to remain in the class—into an existing hybrid class I was teaching at Drexel, taking advantage of the electronic community of the existing course. In 2004, when Belarus's dictator abruptly shut down the European Humanities University (for being too Western), members of the university fled, many to nearby Lithuania. Despite the obvious problems that the school's closing caused, many stranded students were still able to take courses online. One student told the *Chronicle of Higher Education*, "I have three different virtual classes, and every week I write a paper and send it off by e-mail" (MacWilliams, par. 13). A student living in a small town on the Rio Grande in Texas was the only one in his seven-person senior class interested in certain courses, and he was able to take them virtually through the Star Schools Program (Withrow 3). Smith told another story, of a husband and wife with three children who are trying to improve their lives and are able to do so via online learning (vii).

Hearing and living through stories like these, I realize the humanistic potential of this environment. Writing teachers have a unique opportunity because writing-centered online courses allow instructors and students to interact in ways beyond content delivery. They allow students to build a community through electronic means. Perhaps for some—but not all!—such a community will never wholly replace the interactions of an onsite class, but for students whose options are limited, these electronic communities can build the social and professional connections that constitute some of education's real value.

I am aware of the pitfalls of the online environment, and by that I mean the broader dangers of becoming dependent on digital tools for some of the most meaningful aspects of our lives, including education. Marshall McLuhan recounted an Eastern proverb about a man who would not use a lever to do his work, saying, "I have heard my teacher say that whoever uses machines does all his work like a machine. He who does his work like a machine grows a heart like a machine, and he who carries the heart of a machine in his breast loses his simplicity. He who has lost his simplicity becomes unsure in the strivings of his soul. Uncertainty in the strivings of the soul is something which does not agree with honest sense. It is not that I do not know of such things; I am ashamed to use them" (63). In the pre-iPod and Google days, Billie Wahlstrom was blunt about this view of technology: "The computer-supported literacy that students develop may prepare them for an exploitative environment rather than protect them from it" (185). There is a long tradition of suspicion of technology; more than half a century ago, Siegfried Giedeon said, "Never has mankind possessed so many instruments for abolishing slavery. But the promises of a better life have not been kept" (715). More recently, Langdon Winner, in his aptly named chapter "Mythinformation," said of the 1970s and 1980s computer revolution, "Once again, those who push the plow are told they ride a golden chariot" (115). Indeed, you don't have to be a **Luddite** to think that many who have sprinted headlong into the technological future seem enthralled by digital technology to the point of risking being used by the technologies instead of the other way around.

However, caution about technology is not an excuse for inaction. Some compositionists have argued that those of us in writing studies have been too passive regarding technologies, with a few groundbreakers as exceptions. In discussing machine scoring of student writing, for instance, Haswell said bluntly, "Composition teachers had come late to the analysis of language by computer" ("Automatons" 61). As a result, according to Haswell, we have witnessed the increased use of artificial intelligence assessment tools and the seemingly uncontrollable growth of standardized testing. In the introduction to their book, Harrington, Rickly, and Day wrote that if those interested in writing do not get involved with technological development, "we will have no control over the educational resources that are developed" (7). We cannot become so concerned with the negative aspects of technologies, particularly educational technologies, that we miss their potential for us and for our students. Using technology tools in the composition class space can help us, as a field, lend a smarter, more humanistic approach to these learning technologies. This is the view advocated by Andrew Feenberg, whose *critical theory of technology* includes refusing to let technology represent an unavoidable destiny, instead calling for a reconstruction of technology that allows it to work in conjunction with cultural forces rather than control us (14, 127). Walter Ong applied a similar line of thinking to the relationship between language and technology, saying that since the world has been technologized, "there is no effective way to criticize what technology has done with it without the aid of the highest technology available" (80). Throughout this book, I describe reasons for using technological means to teach writing that I hope will resonate with the reasons many of us became teachers of writing and the humanities in the first place.

The online environment also provides us with an opportunity specifically because of the subject matter of the writing course. This is an interesting twist. During the past few years, almost all higher education publications have described the concerns of faculty about placing their course materials online, as the faculty then could perhaps be replaced by anyone with some knowledge of the subject matter (Maguire). Feenberg, in "Distance Learning: Promise or Threat?" voiced the same fears a decade ago. Not so in composition. In his composition classic *Themes, Theories, and Therapy*, Albert Kitzhaber observed that writing teachers "are the most complicated and versatile of all teaching machines" and are unlikely to be replaced (92). Our constant efforts to work with student texts are unique and irreplaceable, and our model of technology use can be perhaps the most humanistic in the academy. For instance, Smith described with considerable expertise how to set up and teach a course, but for her and for most other teaching disciplines, the pedagogical paradigm is clear in her discussion about responding to student messages: "I did not want to become a personal tutor to twenty-five individual students, a highly inefficient use of time" (86). That "inefficient use of time" is at the foundation of the way that writing instructors work with and improve their students' writing. The technology can allow us to hone that role even further.

A Different Student Population

Finally, students have changed, as has our culture. In the introduction to their book about **blended** learning, D. Randy Garrison and Norman Vaughan were direct: "It is beyond time that higher education institutions recognize the untenable position of holding onto past practices that are incongruent with the needs and demands of a knowledge society" (ix). Indeed, students have unprecedented access to technology. There was a time when I felt uncomfortable making such a general statement, because the United States, not to mention the world, consisted of a stark contrast between technological haves and have nots. This is still true, but some studies, at least in the United States, indicate that access to the Internet is much higher among lower-income children than once commonly believed (Nagel). Our students are becoming increasingly digital, regardless of background. They are open and sometimes disturbingly familiar in the social and informational network of the Web. In talking about the use of "disclosure" Web tools like social networking sites, communications professor Julie Frechette wrote, "The new millennium may be the right time to reexamine our philosophical hesitancies to cross the digital line and engage in pedagogical experimentation online" (par. 6). Indeed, part of the *Why* is that we can place our students in a writing context in which they are comfortable, channeling their vast text production skills into a complementary teaching methodology.

According to a Pew report, "Teens write a lot, but they do not think of their emails, instant and text messages as writing. This disconnect matters because teens believe good writing is an essential skill for success and that more writing instruction at school would help them" (Lenhart, par. 1). We can help them address this disconnect, and I believe we will get continually better at helping them contextualize their "school" writing based on the other types of writing they do in their lives. I recognize the potential for an unsettling paradox here, because introducing layers of technology between us and our students can have negative, and, in the parlance of Edward Tenner, unexpected *revenge effects*, in which the side effects of introducing the technology in the writing classroom could directly counter its benefits (8). However, the introduction of layers of technological infrastructure to students' writing education may not complicate their learning, but instead place it within contexts with which they are comfortable and familiar. Christine Hult and Ryan Richins cited studies that 93 percent of thirteen- to seventeen-year-old Internet users also use **IM** (instant messaging) to communicate with peers (par. 1). Teachers often view technology as a distraction, but that's because our teaching is at odds with the e-environment. I, too, can be annoyed when students "do screens" while in my onsite classrooms, but think about it: in our writing classes, while we are talking, they are often diligently writing away—and yet we see this as an obstacle (Slager). The text-based e-environment is an increasingly familiar environment for students. Tom Lavazzi talked about "pedagogic 'happenings'" (127) while students surf the Web; in short, we can teach them while they are there.

Who Are You?

The final question is this: Who are *you*? My target audience for this book is teachers who have taught writing—mainly, although not necessarily exclusively, first-year composition—in onsite classes and are now, for one reason or another, going to teach writing online, in a hybrid environment, or in an environment with many digital tools. I wrote this book for you as a practical, helpful guide to the nuances of the OWcourse. Reader, in my imagination you have several traits. Here is how I picture you, my *primary audience* for this book:

◆ You are an earnest and interested teacher of writing.

- ◆ You may be nervous about teaching online, but you also are meeting this challenge with some enthusiasm.

- ◆ You feel that you will eventually get comfortable with the technology, but right now you need some help getting started. That is, you have the will to move your teaching online, but you are not sure how to work in this environment.

- ◆ You don't consider yourself a Luddite, but you do not necessarily have tremendous technological knowledge. You use email and the Web and word processing, and you are more than willing to give technology tools a chance.

- ◆ You have *some* patience in understanding that it takes time to learn to migrate your classes online, yet you are willing to see how this shift affects your teaching and the learning of your students.

- ◆ You don't have easy, regular access to a course designer; in other words, you will create and design much of the course.

A *secondary audience* is faculty and administrators who train faculty to teach using technology. This book offers a particular approach, as described above, and may present you with some new training tactics. A *tertiary audience* is those who are interested in how different technology tools are being used to improve the writing classroom environment, regardless of discipline. In fact, I think that the electronic writing environment may open up some of the most interesting writing opportunities for those trying to use writing in electronic **WID** (writing in the disciplines) or WAC courses. Although this book seems to feature technology, at its foundation it is about writing instruction. Throughout, I reinforce my beliefs that in the spectrum of teaching, writing instruction is its own peculiar teaching animal, and although it may not always be perceived that way, writing is difficult to teach. Some things we assume about teaching writing are challenged when we move to an online environment. While we draw on the foundational ideas we have always used, we can also find new ways to instruct students about writing strategies, manage the flow of documents, read and respond to student writing, and engage in dialogue with our students.

Making the transition to teaching writing online can be nerve-wracking. Initially (as when you first started teaching f2f) you will feel that there is always something more to do. Sure, you will feel your novicehood acutely, and you'll have the sense that you don't know all of the slick, complex tech tools that you should know to teach effectively. But you will become comfortable in this environment. Once you do, you can allow your teaching creativity to be complemented by the various online tools. The results are often fascinating.

Not for Everyone

It's important to be up front: teaching online will not appeal to everyone. I want you, the teacher, to understand that before we proceed. There are ramifications in the move to online writing that we cannot ignore. You may be asked to teach online writing for reasons that have nothing to do with pedagogy. Perhaps convenience is paramount. Maybe for your school, the decision is driven by finances, and freeing up class space saves money. Sarah Carr, in the *Chronicle of Higher Education,* explained that the recent growth of online courses is motivated by both the desire to offer students flexibility and "the sometimes mistaken belief that online courses can be delivered more cheaply when compared to face-to-face (f2f) courses" (A4). Perhaps the move to online education at your school is motivated by a desire to fragment full-time faculty and use less expensive, disempowered part-timers. Those of us interested in this area will be forced to contend with these issues as online instruction becomes more popular and easier to deliver.

For some students and teachers, online instruction is difficult and even exasperating. I don't want you to be discouraged by initial difficulties when you start teaching online, but I do think we need to be cautious about pushing faculty to teach online and about recommending students for fully online instruction, especially traditionally aged students who live near or on campus or very close. Online writing instruction works well for many students—and for some, even better than traditional onsite learning—but not for all. In Chapter 2, I discuss some strategies to help us make good decisions about which modality is best for teachers and students.

A Word about This Book's Organization

Each chapter of this book takes on a focused area of teaching an OWcourse. Within the structure of the book are several tools to help you navigate your way around:

- *Glossary*. Recurring terms and abbreviations, which appear in bold throughout, can be found in the glossary.
- *Guidelines*. Each chapter has one or more guidelines, which are also listed all together inside the front and back covers. These guidelines are a distillation of the lessons found in each chapter.
- *Pre-term Questions*. At the end of each chapter is a list of questions you can pose before the term starts to help prepare yourself for that first experience teaching online.

The chapters are designed to be short and easily digestible. You'll notice some repetition. For instance, the first appearance of a glossary term is bolded in each chapter because I envision you skipping around, reading the chapters most relevant to your teaching. Several subject areas, such as peer review, are discussed in multiple chapters. Much like the needed redundancy in teaching online, I think this repetition helps to strengthen the message in the book, because I can't be sure where you are going to start and which path you will follow. The material in this book is also complemented with Web resources.

I believe those of us in English departments generally, and writing programs specifically, have a tremendous opportunity before us because of the availability of digital tools to teach writing. This book provides direct, specific answers to your questions about teaching online. I think you will find the move to online instruction worthwhile, and you may well discover that you are helping students write and think in ways previously unimagined.

CHAPTER ONE

Getting Started: Developing Your Online Personality

A key to maximizing the teaching opportunities presented in an online environment is to establish yourself appropriately as an audience for your students. You might assume numerous roles in a class, and these roles shift, but you need to be aware that the way you frame yourself will influence how your students write throughout the course.

In providing a practical approach to teaching writing online, let's start at the beginning, before you ever log on. For me, a weird and unexpected obstacle to planning my first online writing courses was that I initially felt unsure about what kind of persona—what kind of voice—I would have as an online teacher. Elbow once wrote that real voice has the power to make you pay attention and understand (1). Of course, he also knew that voice makes you exposed and vulnerable, and that expressing your real voice can even be painful.

You might have spent years honing your **f2f** classroom persona, and then—*pow!*—you are teaching online—the (no)place where amusing, annoying, and weird teaching mannerisms are preserved, maybe forever. Forget server woes and concerns about carpal tunnel syndrome; when I first embarked on teaching an online composition course, my main worry was how I would conduct myself "in front" of the online students. Those first few message posts, that initial homepage announcement, the introductory email—I realized that the text of those messages created a personality, and I felt great pressure to craft that persona the right way. Would I greet them with "Dear members of English 101"? How about "Dear students"? How about "Hi everyone"?

Or "What's up"? Could I think of a slick sign-off, something better than the stuffy *Professor Warnock*? Would I use slang and **IM** shortcuts?

The online *you* will shape itself during your first term, and don't be surprised if it's different from the onsite classroom *you*. As Sherry Turkle, Julian Dibbell, and others who study online communities have discovered, the personality we adopt to communicate textually in the electronic realm might differ from the way we customarily think of ourselves. As writing teachers, this difference can be a good thing and can help us reconceptualize ourselves.

> **Guideline 4**: Before you get started teaching your first OW-course, think carefully about your online teaching personality—and realize that representation of yourself may change when you teach online.

Different Voices

Although you should avoid overthinking this to the point of paralysis, a number of useful approaches exist to help you think about the kind of voice and persona you will use in your course. Naturally, we develop a personality, perhaps even a stage presence of sorts, when we teach in general. In her book, *Discussion-Based Online Teaching to Enhance Student Learning,* Tisha Bender noted the general importance of "maintaining a confident demeanor" for teachers, observing, "With an enjoyment of and competence in writing, this same sort of enthusiasm can be conveyed online, not only through your choice of words, but also through your responsiveness to your students" (53). Many of us teach writing because we like writing and are skilled at it; you have a great chance to demonstrate your skills in the online environment.

I take a closer look at online conversations and the role you can play in them in Chapter 8, but since the foundation of my approach is having an **asynchronous** textual presence in the course that will extend across much of your communication to students, I discuss briefly here how you might shape that presence. In *Facilitating Online Learning,* a book that provides numerous useful structures for conducting online conversations, George Collison and his coauthors described six different voices you can use as a moderator of online conversations: *generative guide, conceptual facilitator, reflective guide, personal muse, mediator,* and *role play* (106). They also described three key facilitator roles that you can take in an online environment: *guide on the side, instructor* or *project leader,* and *group process facilitator* (33). In Chapter 8, I define each of these voices and roles and demonstrate how they can be enacted in a message board conversation, but perhaps most useful here is the idea that there are distinct, different ways of presenting yourself to a class. You will not know them all initially; as with all teaching, you'll find things in yourself that will surprise you.

You as Audience

Why is it worth spending time before the term starts to think over your online voice? This idea of "framing" yourself is so important to the way your class will operate for a simple reason that should resonate with most writing teachers: *audience.* This is a key component of communication, and compositionists have long been thinking about the ramifications of audience and its importance in a successful writing class experience. For instance, in an influential article in 1984, Lisa Ede and Andrea Lunsford asked, "To what degree should teachers stress audience in their assignments and discussions?" (155). In the online writing class, you might be surprised to discover that (possibly for the first time) you are a *real* audience for your students' writing. I don't mean to downplay the audience role we often play for their essays, themes, papers, and compositions in onsite teaching; but our large, high-stakes writing assignments can sometimes be so artificial, so detached from anything in the students' experiences, so confoundingly difficult, that they don't create the kind of real writer-audience relationship that characterizes the writing students will do in practically every other aspect of their lives. We are still often, sometimes despite our best efforts, the unapproachable sage who knows so much about the topic at hand that the poor students feel they have nothing left to say. Even several decades ago, Moshe Cohen and Margaret Riel argued that assignments that work better "to contextualize students' work" are needed in distance writing courses (143). Not only can assignments help with this, but so can the communication modality.

You may discover a marked difference in their writing when students are constantly writing to you in a *transactional*, get-things-done manner similar to that described by Britton and his coauthors (88): students are writing as participants. This kind of writing can predominate in your course, especially in the multi-audience message board space of the online class. Sure, we have all received emails (or notes) from students who missed class, felt they were graded unfairly, or didn't understand the assignment. But in the online class, almost *all* of these student comments come via writing, potentially taking writing instruction to another level. Students no longer write just at assignment time. They must always be thinking about their writing practices in their course interactions. You are standing in the virtual midst of the students, writing away to them. And they are responding to you and to each other. Who do you want that audience to be? If you aren't careful, you run the risk of being someone you do not want to be, and that someone might hamper your students' ability to develop their writing in your class.

Some Voices and Roles You Do Not Want

Just as there are voices and roles you will want to develop in the class, there are those you will want to avoid. Here are some less-than-ideal audience personas that you might assume, perhaps gradually, when you teach online—and the potential consequences of each:

- ◆ **Unapproachable sage.** If you assume this role, you will notice that every time you comment to your students on the message boards, the conversation withers. Students will be saying, in effect, "Well, the teacher feels *that* way. I guess there's nothing left to say." Student questions via email might seem stilted or confusing, as students struggle to say something worthwhile to the mighty genius running their class.

◆ **Apathetic drone.** Students will quickly catch on if you're not interested in their course conversations, or if you are too busy or preoccupied to respond to their emails. Although they don't need your constant presence to have good conversations (see Chapter 8), if you are clearly detached, their posts and class writing will reflect that. In extreme cases, students in such courses might test you by cutting and pasting responses from week to week, or by inserting nonsense in the midst of their posts. Yes, this really happens.

◆ **Chum.** Before you know it, students are calling you "dude" in their email greetings. They are cursing each other out on the message boards. Maybe you are fine with that. But be careful of letting too much informality creep into written conversations. Remember: your object is to teach them. No doubt many students can run circles around us when it comes to writing informally—they do it *all the time*. Our job (or at least a good part of it for what Douglas Rushkoff first called the *screenagers* we now teach) is to channel and crank up the skills they have learned from all of the **informal writing**—texting, emailing, and using social networking sites—they have been doing, often since they were quite small. Many young teachers, especially in the naturally chummy first-year writing class, note how difficult it can be to become *teacher* with a capital *T*. I'm not recommending that you become the unapproachable sage, but remember that your job is to teach them something about writing. Plain and simple: not every message is appropriate for every context, and that is a valuable rhetorical lesson they can learn in the e-environment.

I learned this the hard way teaching onsite. I always felt it would be better if students were comfortable with me, that such comfort could better power their writing. So I always asked them to call me Scott. Several years ago, in my first term teaching at Penn State Lehigh Valley, I introduced myself as Scott. But I was nearly twenty years older than most of my students—and I must admit, however begrudgingly, that with silver hair, I looked at *least* twenty years older than them. So it turned out that many students wouldn't call me *anything* because, it seemed, they were uncomfortable with Scott. For a variety of reasons, these students were not well served by writing to their pal, Scott. Their expectations were upended by my efforts to be informal, so I changed my address to Professor Warnock, where I continue to reside today.

◆ **Fool.** I sometimes wonder if the danger of appearing the fool scares teachers away from the online environment. Writing is difficult; that's all there is to it. In the **OWcourse**, you, the teacher, will write, write, and write some more. What if you make an ugly mistake? Nothing I can say will assuage all your concerns: when you write thousands and thousands of words in an online writing class, you will make mistakes. But if you are perpetually sloppy and lazy with your posts—not proofing them, a task you will no doubt require of your students—then indeed, your students may lose respect for you, regardless of whether you can write expertly when you want to. You can take a number of approaches to this issue. I sometimes turn it into a teaching moment: anyone who catches me making a mistake and identifies the mistake gets extra credit. Of course, I avoid making mistakes as best I can, but I estimate conservatively that I write more than 30,000 words to my students each term. Mistakes are inevitable. However, if you communicate in a sloppy fashion, your students will catch on quickly and might not take you seriously. In a worst-case scenario, your poor public writing in the course could come back to haunt you at grading time.

♦ **Harsh critic.** In the OWcourse, often you are not the only person to read many of the messages you write to students; much of your communication will be on semipublic spaces in the class. If you harshly criticize your students, you could lose them for the rest of the term. You should take the role of teacher to guide and sometimes correct them, but if you slam them, especially in front of the others, you could create a negative environment. This is tough, because you might appear to be a harsh critic due to the nature of textual communications: sometimes the words just don't come out as intended.

No doubt you could come up with more audience roles that might be troublesome for your students. At times, you might fall into one or more of these roles, but if one of them begins to dominate your communication during the term, you will likely lose some students.

> **Guideline 5**: Think about the possible negative roles that you can take as an online interlocutor, and try not to let one of those roles dominate your communication style in the course.

Using Icebreakers to Help Shape Yourself in the Class

Just as you might in an onsite class, you can start getting to know your students, and shaping yourself to them, with introductory icebreakers. I use a first-week icebreaker in all my courses; this always serves broader pedagogical goals than just filling up a message board (or spending the time f2f). In a **hybrid** course, you may choose to have students introduce themselves both onsite and online, noting any differences in how they present themselves in each environment. The following is an icebreaker I use in my classes. Note that I not only require students to post their icebreaker, but I also ask them to post a response to someone else.

```
SUBJ: Who are you?
Dear members of English 102:
I'd like to get to know you a bit and, perhaps more
importantly, for you to get to know each other. So
could you please let us know a few things about
yourself?
```

- Tell us who you are, where you're from, and what your major is/interests are.

- Post a picture of one thing—and it can be any-thing—that you have that helps demonstrate an important aspect of you, then describe that thing. (Think of it this way: if we were in a face-to-face classroom and I asked you to bring something that demonstrates an important aspect of you, what would you bring and why?)

- What are some topics that you like to debate or that you have strong feelings about? (Note: You don't even have to reveal which side you're on; just tell us what the topic/subject is.)

```
Please provide your email address, and sign this
post with your name.

Feel free to reply back to each other on this Dis-
cussion thread, and please note that this post is
separate from your other Discussion requirements
this week.

Looking forward to hearing about you,
Prof. Warnock
```

Here is an icebreaker I use in my hybrid courses:

```
Subj: Getting to know each other
Hi everyone,
As I've said several times, welcome to English 101.
    As you've no doubt gathered from the course syl-
labus, the message boards will play a big role in
what we do this term. Let's get to know each other a
little on this medium before our first class.
```

> We're all going to walk into a real classroom on
> Thursday. Answer this on this message board thread
> as a way of getting to know each other: "When I walk
> into class on Thursday, I'd like everyone to say,
> 'Oh, that's the person who ____.'" Then briefly ex-
> plain why you would want us to think of you in that
> way.
>
> Some of you will no doubt have simple, straight-
> forward answers. That's fine. Others of you will have
> a lot more to say. Some may want to pick a funny de-
> tail, hobby they like, or noteworthy aspect of their
> personality. Others will want to say several things
> about themselves. It's very much up to you.
>
> Regardless, please make sure that you've posted
> by Tuesday evening so we all get a chance to know
> each other. This post counts as an "official post,"
> so make sure you check the syllabus to see the rules
> for posts ("rules" sounds so heavy-handed—maybe I
> should call them "guidelines"?).
>
> Please let me know if you have any questions (you
> can post them here or on the "Questions about as-
> signments" thread).
> I'm looking forward to reading a little about you,
> Prof. Warnock

Icebreakers help students describe themselves, but they should serve another purpose regarding your identity in the class. During that first week of class, I stay pretty busy because I respond in some detail to *every* icebreaker response. I try to build a connection with each student: "Oh, you like classic rock? I am a big Zeppelin fan" or "Vonnegut is one of my favorite authors too" or "I used to live near Voorhees." Because the students don't actually see me, I try to create links between us, not just to develop a sense of camaraderie (although this is important), but to create an audience for them. The "black box" of audience can be a problem for students in an onsite class, so imagine how this might be exacerbated when they never see the instructor. I chose the icebreakers earlier to demonstrate the kind of persona I wish to take in the course.

> **Guideline 6:** Start off your term with some type of electronic icebreaker to help everyone get to know one another and understand how the textual interaction in the class will work.

At Some Point, You Need to Jump In

Although I have emphasized spending time and thought on your online personality, I want to close this chapter with some slightly contrary advice. Looking back on my own OWcourse teaching experiences, I realize that in an online class, as in teaching onsite (or almost any other endeavor), you cannot know exactly how you are going to present yourself or predict the effect of that presentation on your students; at some point you have to just jump in there. Plain and simple, worries about perfecting your voice cannot obstruct you from just getting started. Carol Berkenkotter once remarked that writing under too many constraints is a formula for writer's block (34), and I think the same dynamic is at work here: as we advise frustrated, timid, or bored writing students, one of the main tricks to writing is that you must just get started. Although I know this is true, each time I start teaching an online writing class, I feel the slight nervousness as introductory emails and message board posts come flowing in. Who am I? Better yet: who do I want to be? Ultimately, I realize that if I ask too many questions—create too many constraints—then I will not write or teach at all. My identity is still taking shape, and when I think about this more broadly, it shouldn't be surprising.

In *Engaging the Online Learner*, Rita-Marie Conrad and J. Ana Donaldson cited M. Knowles, who said that "setting up an appropriate learning climate is key to establishing a successful learning experience" (qtd. in Conrad and Donaldson 46). So if you want a slick signature that will save you some keystrokes, create one. (I am still working on this. *ProfW* is the best I can do right now.) Think about the level of formality in your greetings and complimentary closings—perhaps you will use different levels depending on the purpose of your message—but know that until you start writing to your students in the heat of the class, you won't be sure of your teaching persona and the little words that will define it. I revisit the idea of audience throughout this book. The online environment provides a fascinating opportunity for you to heighten and refine your definition of *audience* in a classroom. If you take hold of this opportunity, you will find ways to expand what you do as a teacher of writing.

Pre-term Questions

◆ *What kind of audience would be useful for you to adopt for your student writers?* Thinking about this will help you better frame your communications to your students and help them understand you better as an audience for their writing.

◆ *How do you want to address students?* Your textual relationship with your students will be influenced significantly by how you present yourself, which begins with how you address them.

◆ *How do you want students to address you and each other?* On the message boards, will it be "Dear students" or "Hi class" or "Hey all"? Are you Scott or Dr. Warnock or ProfW? These slight markers of difference can mean a lot for the course communications.

◆ *Are your class mores, or rules, articulated in your syllabus?* If you describe these expectations in your syllabus, students will appreciate that you have helped them understand how to interact in what may be a new way, especially for an academic class environment. This is discussed in detail in Chapter 5.

◆ *What kind of icebreaker should you create?* Develop an icebreaker for week one that allows students to introduce themselves to the class and to you. Even in a hybrid, that icebreaker should at least partially take place via writing in an electronic space.

CHAPTER TWO

Online or Hybrid?

This chapter investigates differences between teaching fully online and in hybrid or blended courses and offers suggestions about when one modality might be preferable.

This book broadly conceptualizes teaching writing *online* as using technology tools to teach writing, and the term **OW-course** means teaching anchored in these tools. Even if you see the advantages of using online tools more rigorously to teach first-year writing, you might still be reluctant or unable to immerse yourself and your students in a fully virtual classroom.

This is where **hybrid courses** show considerable promise. Hybrid or **blended courses** (I prefer *hybrid;* based on an informal survey that colleague Robin Zeff and I conducted on the Writing Program Administrators **Listserv** [WPA-L] in 2008, most writing programs appear to use that term) are becoming increasingly popular for a variety of reasons. They can reduce costs, allow students to self-pace through courses, and even improve retention, according to a study of large classes by George Marsh, Anna McFadden, and Barrie Jo Price. *Hybrid* can mean a number of things, but I define it here as a course that is offered partly onsite and partly online. In its simple form, you teach half the course as you normally would, and the other half would be migrated into an online environment. For writing courses, hybrids offer a great alternative to the onsite and fully online course experiences. Hybrid courses may offer optimized teaching and learning opportunities for teachers and students who are not truly "distant" from each other. Garrison and Vaughan wrote that the "greatest possibility of recapturing the ideals of higher education is through redesigning blended learning" (x). Bender noted that hybrids push "back the classroom walls," allowing students to conduct conversations after class has ended and faculty to prepare materials for the next onsite class, and that with these types of courses "different learning styles and methods can be accommodated" (xvii). With a hybrid, in a sense, you can maximize some of the best aspects of both teaching worlds.

Will Students Learn as Well?

I will touch on this topic only briefly, because many studies indicate that students learn as well in hybrid or online classes as in onsite classes. The *No Significant Difference Phenomenon* website lists hundreds of studies "that document *no significant differences* (NSD) in student outcomes between alternate modes of education delivery" (Western Cooperative for Educational Telecommunications, screen 1). To the mild frustration of those invested in online learning, these studies continue to be done, replicating the result that students are educated at least as well in online courses. For instance, a 2008 study reported by the *Chronicle of Higher Education* found that students appear to learn as well in hybrid courses as in **f2f** courses (Young).

The evidence is persuasive that student learning is unaffected by online or hybrid modalities, although the experience might *feel* different for teachers and students—leading to incidents such as the drop rates in our first term of offering online courses at Drexel. The job ahead of us, then, is to work on improving the delivery of these courses, confident of the quality of the education we are providing for our students in OWcourses.

Hybrid versus Online for Teachers and Students

You may not be in a position to decide between fully online and hybrid courses, but if you are, it's wise to view your move into the online teaching environment as a progression that will begin with teaching a hybrid first. We have done this at Drexel, where teachers often teach hybrids first before going fully online. The obvious logic is that teachers can make a gradual shift to using online tools, building their comfort with teaching and communicating with students through electronic means.

> **Guideline 7**: If your students live nearby, you may have the option of offering fully online or hybrid courses. Based on your own level of comfort as you enter the digital teaching realm, you should determine whether you first want to teach in a hybrid or a fully online environment.

Of course, hybrid course "gateways" are not going to work in many situations. You might need online classes because your students are far away. You might be running out of brick-and-mortar classrooms (this is not the preferred reason to embark on online writing courses: pedagogy and student learning should always be the driving forces). Or you might simply teach at an online institution.

At Drexel, we began an initiative in 2004 to offer online courses directly from the Department of English and Philosophy, and we offered fully online writing courses all year, including for our on-campus first-term students. After a year, we reassessed what we were doing and made some changes. The major shift was the introduction of hybrid courses, which immediately broadened the number of teachers who were interested in online writing instruction and able to try working in that area. Although we maintain fully online courses in our second- and third-term courses in our three-course sequence (and a for-profit branch of Drexel called Drexel eLearning offers online courses all the time), in our department we stopped offering fully online first-term courses to traditionally aged students living on campus. Why? We felt that although we were developing solid and rigorous online pedagogies, first-term, on-campus students might have trouble if they viewed the online writing course as an easy way out—simply a way not to get up and go to class. Even in the small number of fully online sections we offered, the add and drop rates and grades in these classes sent a signal that students were not being well served. It seemed that many who enrolled in an online class were unprepared for that type of course. (For instance, in my onsite 101 in fall 2004, I had an 8 percent drop rate; for my online course that term, I had a 44 percent drop rate.)

Fully online and hybrid courses both offer scheduling flexibility for students, but students who enroll in those courses need to consider things ranging from their own ability to be a self-starter to the reliability of and access to computers (this plural is deliberate, as they need to have access to backup technology). Hybrid courses provide students with the weekly structure of seeing (and being accountable) to a teacher while still enjoying the advantages of online tools. Students who are motivated and prepared can thrive in the fully online course and receive the full benefits of operating in a completely textual class environment.

The main points that underlie our instructional efforts are these: Are we offering courses that teachers can realistically teach well? Are we providing students with effective learning opportunities? No matter how you decide to approach the use of online tools, you must keep in mind not only *how* you will deliver the courses but also *why*. Without a solid answer to the *why* question, you will want to rethink the rationale behind your use of electronic tools.

Stepping into Online Teaching through Hybrids

If you are approaching your first OWcourse with some trepidation, and you have the choice to teach a hybrid first, here are some ways to smooth your path to fully online instruction.

Organization

There is less pressure for you to organize a hybrid course. Half of the course will be conducted in a way that is familiar to teachers who work onsite. Teachers can step into online modes by envisioning what they will do in that second half of the week when their students are meeting online or conducting activities online.

Communication

As I discuss repeatedly in this book, one of the biggest pressures in teaching writing online is rethinking your communication with students. In a fully online class, you may never have the opportunity for that off-the-cuff comment that so strongly characterizes your onsite teaching style, and you don't get to catch students walking out of the room to remind them of something. And, of course, you must write. This emphasis on simply writing is a stressor that can be significantly lessened in the hybrid environment. Although many hybrid courses seem to be a fifty-fifty split between online and onsite modalities, you can decide what constitutes each half. For instance, in a hybrid, you can use the onsite part of the course for much of your instructional communication, including discussions about tasks, guidelines, expectations, and due dates. Having received their instructions from you, students can then venture into the online portion of the course to do the rest of their work for the week.

Content

Many tools can help you, yet it can be daunting to think about the way you will deliver *all* course material and lessons to students in a fully online environment. Hybrids allow you an opportunity to still deliver some course content in the familiar f2f way.

Response

The first time you receive a list of electronic files instead of a stack of papers can be quite a jolt, but the hybrid environment allows you to control the way you receive, respond to, and return your students' writing: paper or bytes?

Grading

As I mention in Chapter 12, online teaching should lead you to rethink the way you weight and grade assignments, but obviously, in a hybrid you can conduct at least half of your grading practices (for example, quizzes) as you normally would.

Time

I believe that common arguments about the extensive amount of time it takes to teach online compared with onsite are often exaggerated, and some studies support this view (see Hislop and Ellis). Still, for the person who is unsure about teaching with technology, there can be a difference. Moving into hybrids first should lessen this disparity, as you need to think about migrating only half of your materials online to work in that environment.

Comfort

Obviously, much of the above boils down to this: if you are worried about teaching online for the first time, a hybrid class will allow you to stay closer to your comfort zone. You can ease yourself into using online tools, finding what works for you and what does not.

Communicate with Students about Online and Hybrid Courses

To communicate clearly with students about what online and hybrid classes are all about, you should have material on a website that students can access if they have questions—setting it up as an **FAQ** is ideal. You also might want to work with your admissions staff to provide materials about hybrid and online modalities in the information supplied to incoming students. For example, on our department website (Drexel University, Department of English and Philosophy) Drexel includes a description of the online and hybrid courses offered in its Freshman Writing Program. Resources like this can help students make informed decisions about the kind of instruction they will receive. Without them, students will hit us with a lot of questions. And despite what we may think about the high-level skills and technophilia of our screenagers, many may view online and hybrid courses as risky options as they settle into the new world of college. Their parents might also feel that online and hybrid courses cut corners; they might encourage their children to take courses with an instructor always present, thinking that this is what the traditional college experience is about.

You can calm these fears with solid communication materials that illustrate the commitment your program has made to online and hybrid courses. You might choose to include evidence, such as the way that hybrid and online courses have worked for students: retention data, grades, and workload information. For instance, at Drexel we supported our efforts to offer online courses in our first year by using midterm surveys indicating that students were as satisfied with their online courses as they were with their onsite courses.

The decision to teach online or hybrid might not be in your control, whether you are an instructor, program coordinator, or director. With the proper training and support, you'll be able to offer fully online courses immediately at your institution. But if you can offer hybrid courses as a gateway to fully online courses, this may provide a number of advantages for you and other teachers. The gentler progression from onsite to hybrid, then to fully online, could result in teachers spending their time refining and innovating rather than worrying about technology issues.

What about the students? Online learning is becoming more common. At Drexel we shielded traditionally aged students from first-time fully online classes, but after that, we felt students should have the opportunity to take fully online courses when they desired. And we should not privilege the onsite experience as the most personal. As Bender noted, "Online classes might be very welcome to those who have been typically used to very large lecture halls, as they might benefit from more personal attention." She added that in place of online courses, hybrids "also might provide wonderful opportunities for the discussion from the campus class to spill over online" (169). I will sum up my main point in another guideline.

> **Guideline 8:** Students learn and teachers teach in a variety of ways. Online and hybrid courses should be viewed as ways of expanding your learning offerings at your institution, but all modalities need not be available to all students at all times.

Pre-term Questions

◆ *What kinds of courses are offered at your institution?* Hybrid courses already may be an option for you. Is that the way you would prefer to teach?

- *What kinds of training opportunities are available?* Regardless of the modality, you need to find out what resources are available. Faculty might not realize that support is right next door.

- *Would it help if you could transition from onsite to hybrid first?*

- *With whom can you speak outside your institution about teaching modality?* Some of the websites listed as resources in this book can help you make connections with others teaching in the online environment.

CHAPTER THREE

Tech Tools and Strategies: Use Only What You Need

This chapter reviews basic learning technologies to help you understand what technology you will need in your OWcourse. We'll also take a brief look ahead at a few technologies and systems that could influence online writing instruction.

M any technology tools exist to help you teach writing online. Of course, this can be an obstacle when you get started, because the possibilities can be simply overwhelming. You can't help but feel that you are leaving something out. This is why I approach teaching an **OWcourse** as doing the simple things first—things that you already have mastered in your onsite teaching—and then finding matching technologies.

> **Guideline 9**: Don't be any more complicated technologically than you have to be. The foundation of your class, even in the most high-tech environment, is still your own personal teaching ability and imagination. Build from that as you investigate the many tools that can help you teach online.

As you get more comfortable, you can investigate the interesting world of technology teaching tools, which range from bells and whistles to methods that will fundamentally change the way you teach in any modality. Remember, though, that an obligation in online instruction is "making sure that all participants have the necessary skill level with the communication tools that will be used during the course" (Conrad and Donaldson 37). You can start with yourself.

Getting the Right Mix

You will want to create a balance in your use of technological tools. As a new teacher in the online setting, you can start your technological decision making with a straightforward table like the following one. This will help you map out the technologies you will need to master and how much training you will need. It is key to get the first column right, because from there you determine the pedagogical needs of your classroom.

Pedagogical need	Technology for that purpose	Availability	Training? Your learning curve
Communicate with individual students	I will use email.	Students and I will all have email.	I am familiar with normal email. If I want to use **CMS** email, I might need training.
Establish conversation between students, and teacher and students, about readings and course lessons	I want to use message boards.	Message boards are part of our CMS; all classes are automatically set up in CMS at start of term.	I need some training in setting up and grading posts.
Place for students to submit work	Final drafts of major projects via CMS drop-boxes; rough drafts via email or message boards.	Easy to access: see above for CMS and email.	Email is no problem. I can learn by myself how to use the simple assignment drop boxes in CMS.
Class announcements	Email; homepage of CMS.	All easily available.	Email is no problem. I need a quick lesson in using CMS announcements.
Facilitate peer review	I'm not sure yet how I will do this.	I may try to match up students and have them review each other via the message boards.	I need training. I will look at resources on facilitating online peer review.

Deliver course lessons	I have Word and PowerPoint files with some of my course lessons about writing.	I know these materials can be posted on the course CMS.	I know how to post files. I may explore using learning modules, for which I would need training.
Respond to student writing	I will use email attachments of electronic files for final drafts and message boards for rough drafts.	Technologies to help me respond are easily available.	I need background in message boards; are there better ways to respond electronically?
Deliver course grades	I will use the gradebook in CMS.	Easily accessible.	I need background training in using the gradebook.
Create audiovisual materials for students	I will look into the software and hardware available to create these materials.	I know that audiovisual materials can be posted on CMS. I'm unsure how to acquire the software to record such materials.	I don't know how to create these materials, but I'm interested in learning.
Facilitate group projects	Message boards can help; my CMS may have group functions.	These functions are available in CMS.	I need training to use group functions.

This list can become increasing complex, and you can add to it as you progress. In the beginning of your first term, try to keep it simple, working from the pedagogical needs described in the first column. In each term following your first, you might want to add one or two new technologies. This will allow you to continue experimenting with technologies in a controlled manner. You could even create another column in which you rank the relative complexity of the technologies you are employing.

Your Core Technology Structure

To help simplify things during your first term teaching an OWcourse, I offer several basic technologies for your learning environment. I can't stress enough that expanding on these basics is only a function of your own creativity. Remember that I approach the OWcourse with a particular slant; there are other possibilities for teaching writing online.

CMS

Keep it simple: for many online writing teachers, the core technological structure of your class will start with your CMS, and probably that will be provided by your institution. That's fine; you should focus on learning the ins and outs of your CMS so the technology you need to teach does not present an ongoing obstacle throughout the term. There are many CMS options, including Angel, Blackboard and Blackboard Vista (formerly WebCT), Desire2Learn, Moodle, and Sakai. Mount Holyoke College has a great website to help you understand differences among various kinds of CMS. It was derived from a similar website by EduTools that provides a place to compare strengths and weaknesses of different kinds of CMS. Maricopa Community Colleges maintains an older but still useful website that includes links to compare a variety of systems, including some that are lesser known. In her book *The Tools for Successful Online Teaching*, Lisa Dawley offered a brief but helpful discussion of various kinds of CMS, pointing out that the basic functions are similar among systems: "While LMSs may vary in appearance or in how some features are used, overall the learning and administrative tools of the LMS are fairly consistent" (12). As your teaching evolves, you might be interested in the interfaces, specific tools, and advantages of a specific CMS, but these systems all offer similar basic functionality, especially for the new teacher: message boards, chat or **whiteboard** space, file access, announcements, group functions, assignment dropboxes (which may include plagiarism checkers), and calendars.

I want to emphasize the value of starting your foray into online teaching of writing with one of these packages. Your goal is to get past the technology and start thinking about teaching. The technology should be relatively transparent and unobtrusive because, frankly, you will have enough to think about as you start teaching online. Why make it more difficult? Use a packaged software that delivers all the tools you need and provides an easy place for your students to meet you and each other online in a relatively protected, private area of the Internet. As you progress, you might find another online structure—perhaps a **wiki** or **blog**—that better meets your needs, but using such an approach from the start will introduce some difficult issues that you will have to solve on your own. Another advantage of using your school's CMS is that when you run into problems, in most cases you will have support.

> **Guideline 10:** In your initial efforts to teach an OWcourse, simplify things by using your campus CMS, and learn only the tools you know you will need.

As an alternative, some textbook publishers now offer CMS-type systems geared specifically to writing courses. Your local company representatives will be eager to show you these often sophisticated tools.

Email

Email can do much of the work for you in an online class. You might be surprised by how much you rely on it and how effective it is: if you think the most valuable thing you can do is interact with your students one-on-one, then email would be a natural, wouldn't it? You can spend a lot of useful time simply being a textual mentor and interlocutor with students via email.

The Web

Remember that in the OWcourse, students almost always have access to the Web. Use that. In their conversations with you and with each other, they should substantiate everything using evidence and research. You have access to countless readings and resources, many of which you can link from within your CMS. Don't forget that students have this perpetual access in the OWcourse.

Phone

It seems quaint to mention, but remember that you can still talk to your students on the phone. The phone continues to evolve as a key communication device, especially for those in our traditionally aged students' generation. Many people who think about technology in education see mobile devices, such as cell phones, becoming increasingly important in educating students, providing a range of unprecedented opportunities (for more on this topic, see the articles by Patricia Thornton and Chris Houser or Giasemi Vavoula et al.). Students can text, receive email, and browse with their increasingly sophisticated phones; we may have to meet them in that world in order to teach them effectively. Ask for students' phone numbers early in the term, and be willing to call them if necessary—and they should feel comfortable calling you.

Some Fancier Options

Audiovisual Technologies

Internet video is improving, in all ways, and the barriers to using AV materials in teaching promise to decrease substantially. Student access might remain an obstacle, but as **Web 2.0** technologies continue to improve, your ability to introduce AV materials in your classes will increase. So in thinking about how to deliver course material, communicate with students, and conduct workshops, AV materials should be in your mindset. There are several ways to create videos for students.

- ◆ Some IT departments on campus have studio-like classroom spaces in which you can record class lessons.
- ◆ You can use desktop video recording software, such as Camtasia.
- ◆ Many computers now come with built-in webcams that make recording easy.

Dissemination of AV files and materials is another matter, often not easily solved because of the large size of the files.

- ◆ At Drexel, we have a sophisticated media server that converts files into user-friendly Web links for students. Students simply click on a link to watch a video on their computers (Drexel University, Information Resources and Technology).

- ◆ Several websites provide ways for you to upload video files. TeacherTube is specifically for educators.

- ◆ You can podcast audio files using **MP3** formats.

- ◆ You can load files onto your CMS.

- ◆ In some cases you can send files via email, but their large size normally makes this problematic.

This is a starter list and nothing more. The expanding technologies of the Web will help us make a similar expansion in our use of AV materials.

Virtual Worlds

The possibilities of virtual worlds did not just begin with the website Second Life. People have been interacting in all kinds of ways in these virtual environments for years. In *My Tiny Life*, Dibbell charts his own increasing absorption in a text-based virtual world. These worlds are now graphically based, and we might be able to educate our students in these environments. In fact, the *Chronicle of Higher Education* has been covering Second Life closely, sometimes critically, but often noting that educators are at the forefront of exploring innovative ways to use virtual worlds and immersive educational environments (Foster).

I am no expert on these environments, but you might imagine intriguing possibilities. As my Drexel colleague in chemistry, Jean-Claude Bradley, has shown in a variety of ways, including on his blog *Useful Chemistry*, teachers can use the virtual environment of Second Life to create stimulating platforms for student learning. Bradley has students and other professional collaborators interacting virtually to attempt to discover a cure for malaria. You can envision ways of using the Second Life environment as a virtual common place for students, and if the past few programs for the Conference on College Composition and Communication (CCCC) are any indication, this is an increasingly promising area for teachers of composition to pursue. In 2007 there were two presentations (on the same panel) about Second Life specifically. In 2009, by my count, there were more than ten.

Games

Many in education circles are enthusiastic about the potential of gaming paradigms in education. Every week I notice more discussion and investigation into ways of using electronic gaming platforms for teachers. This fascinating area is open for development, especially in terms of using gaming concepts in teaching college-level writing.

Rubrics and Response and AI Evaluation Tools

Many tools have been designed to help teachers evaluate writing, and some use an artificial intelligence (AI) foundation. As I mentioned in the introduction, composition has not been aggressive enough in investigating technologies of response, and as a result, those in other areas have developed tools to help evaluate writing. These tools have shortcomings (see Patricia Freitag Ericsson and Richard Haswell's *Machine Scoring of Student Essays* for thoughtful, in-depth essays about these technologies). Yet they may have uses for evaluating short, fact-based writing prompts, even if these kinds of prompts tend to occur more often in content-based courses. In any case, you should be aware that tools exist, such as the following, that claim to be able to read and evaluate student writing: Project Essay Grade, Intelligent Essay Assessor, ACCUPLACER, Criterion, and Qualrus.

Less dramatic, but possibly more helpful in terms of response, are rubric sites, especially RubiStar (although a search for *rubrics writing* turns up thousands of hits). In addition, Waypoint is a Web-based rubric creation software designed to assist teachers in evaluating writing.

Publisher Sites

Book publishers have been hard at work developing electronic tools to complement your classes or even to serve as the basis for an online writing classroom experience. Some of these sites are very good and worth a look, especially in the way they feature Web-based writing environments that allow students to connect easily to advice and guidance in the publishers' handbooks and in the way they use multimedia materials.

To close our brief discussion of technologies, it's worth remembering that although the technologies we use in all aspects of our lives are becoming more robust, these tools do fail. Sometimes the server is down. Sometimes the computer's hardware goes awry. Although many intriguing technologies exist to help, in recommending practices for effective online teaching, John Barber suggests that when using technology, you come up with alternate plans; you cannot assume things will always work (256). This is wise advice, and it applies to introducing anything novel to your class. Once a friend of mine was going to attend my class to serve as guest audience member for class group presentations, but he got a flat tire on the way and never made it. You will need flexibility, but you should also make it clear to students that if they are taking a course in this environment, they must be ready for the various implications of using technology, including the chance that it may fail. The new version of "the dog ate my homework" is "my computer crashed." In my syllabus, as I mention in Chapter 5, I require my online students to make certain they have a backup computer to access, even if only for a day or two. Getting the right technology is not only relevant for us, but for our students too.

Pre-term Questions

- *What is your campus CMS?*

- *Which members of your campus IT department can help you? What training sessions are available to help you become comfortable with the technology?*

- *What are you going to do in your OW course, and what technologies will you need?* Create a table similar to the one on page 20 that begins with your pedagogical needs and translates those needs into a technology tool. As you start out, don't worry about all that you don't know. Start in a comfort zone, and build outward.

CHAPTER FOUR

Course Lessons and Content: Translating Teaching Styles to the OWcourse

An online writing course is different from most other online courses, as much of the content can be student generated. This chapter describes several ways of approaching course content and material in the online environment.

We teach composition in innumerable ways. As a discipline, it brings out enormous teaching creativity and innovation. Interestingly, the content of many writing courses is largely composed of the students' own work. This is a difference from most other paradigms, particularly in e-learning, which focus on content delivery (although often in creative, interactive ways). For instance, one of the central ideas described by Elizabeth Ashburn is that "teaching content that is *central to the discipline* and also relevant to students' lives is a . . . fundamental attribute for designing meaningful learning experiences" (13). Most guides to e-learning *start* with content. For our purposes, I will boil down teaching strategies to several basic approaches that might capture the way teachers approach the lessons and learning in a course:

- ◆ Talking to or lecturing students

- ◆ Posing questions to students in Socratic fashion and having them respond

- ◆ Engaging in conversations: you talk with students, and they talk with each other

- ◆ Having students work in groups

- ◆ Engaging students in a workshop-style or hands-on activity in the classroom space

- ◆ Asking students to engage in unsupervised work outside the classroom

This is a simplified continuum, with overlap among the categories, but it captures the general approaches we might take when we prepare to teach a class. The challenge in the **OWcourse** is to translate these approaches into online teaching. As composition teachers, we may have an inherent advantage, which is another reason that we, among all teachers, should be at the forefront of investigating online teaching possibilities: we are already accustomed to student-centered courses. Smith noted that in online learning, the content focus shifts from the teacher to the content itself (65). As teachers of composition, we are accustomed to that focus being away from us and on the students.

This student-centered approach can make things difficult for us, because the paradigm of many resources and technologies is that of the lecture, or the delivery of information (see Chapter 18 for resources about content delivery). It is *not* the writing-intensive, student-centered course paradigm, which, one might argue, requires a more sophisticated use of technologies similar to the interactive technologies characteristic of **Web 2.0**. Delivering information to students was no doubt one of the early barriers e-learning had to overcome to make it a viable teaching tool, and in many cases educators still rely on that paradigm in their use of instructional technology. Several years ago, Mike Palmquist made this observation:

> Course management systems, despite their growing sophistication, are likely to undergo significant transformations before they adequately meet the needs of writing centers and **WAC** programs. *In most cases, the leading systems are based on metaphors associated with the teacher-centered lecture course, rather than on the more participatory, student-centered writing course.* Emerging systems, however, suggest the promise of systems based on metaphors more compatible with writing centers and WAC programs—metaphors such as small-group discussion, collaborative review sessions, and individual conferences. (screen 13; italics added)

Next, I review various methods of re-creating the teaching categories mentioned earlier, but I distinctly lean toward the use of more student-centered methods in the OWcourse.

Talking to Your Students

You may draw on a variety of course lessons to teach different aspects of writing, ranging from logic to rhetoric to grammar. Your **CMS** can offer many ways to deliver content to students; a CMS is often an electronic version of an old, trusty technology for this purpose: the book. In the OWcourse, we can use many means of one-way transmission of text and other material to students. However, we can augment that delivery—although that might not *always* be necessary—with audio or AV tools that are becoming increasingly prevalent and easy to use. These materials can allow students to self-pace through those materials or to follow an AV presentation.

Most CMS packages provide ways of bundling material into learning modules (Figure 4.1), sometimes called **SCORM** (Sharable Content Object Reference Model). Modules can incorporate a variety of materials grouped together for a particular learning purpose.

According to Smith, online course content should include several components: it should be *chunked* into short learning segments; allow students to review the material; let students pause at

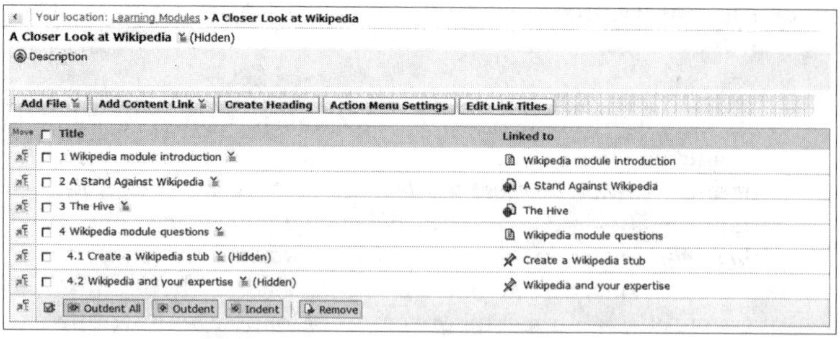

FIGURE 4.1. *Blackboard Vista learning module combining readings, links, and message board conversations.*

any point without going back to the beginning; and provide clear instructions (64–65). These excellent rules of thumb can help you consider how to present your content. Indeed, Smith reinforces the value of **chunking**: "Content presented in one long segment is much less effective for learning than the same content broken down into several smaller segments" (71). One strength of a good CMS is that it provides you with a framework to deliver such material to students in an easy-to-use way.

I speak only briefly here about the model of talking *to* your students; that topic has been covered expertly by others. In fact, it is because I noticed the clear focus on this mode of teaching in most available books and teaching materials that I was inspired to write about teaching writing in an OWcourse. Your course lessons, no matter the form, can be delivered to students in this environment with some work on your part, and perhaps with help from an instructional designer.

Posing Questions to Students in Socratic Fashion and Having Them Respond

This method works well in the online environment, and you can teach in this way with either **asynchronous** or **synchronous** electronic text-based tools. In fact, this teaching method might be served better by chats and other synchronous technologies than by asynchronous tools. I will describe this difference more thoroughly in later chapters.

Some of my best teachers were masters of the Socratic Method of teaching. In particular, I remember my graduate school experiences with Dr. Timothy Martin of Rutgers-Camden. He would warm us up with easy questions, building our confidence and creating classroom energy before delving into the more difficult issues that were the objective of that class lesson. Online, you can use chat for this teaching style. Conferencing technologies allow you to have all students in the same place at the same time, as do Voice over Internet Protocol (VoIP) tools. You could also have these conversations via a message board, **listserv**, **blog**, or **wiki**. Socratic conversations can be built into your message boards: pose simple, direct questions to students initially, and then during the week, work toward a more complex learning goal. This method is described more fully in my Chapter 8 discussion of message boards. However, the Socratic Method can be enhanced by using many of the tools of the online writing class, where there are perhaps even more participatory ways of engaging students than in onsite courses.

Engaging in Conversations: You Talk with Students, and They Talk with Each Other

The potential for online writing instruction comes to the fore here, in our innovative uses of the e-environment to facilitate conversation among our students. We could say that we are meeting students even more effectively in this way because, maturing in the interactive age of Web 2.0, they are increasingly accustomed to having *dialogue* instead of simply being passive recipients of information.

Textual Asynchronous Conversations

I spend much time, particularly in Chapter 8, discussing asynchronous conversations. The message board is front and center, providing an easy-to-use yet pedagogically powerful teaching tool to facilitate student communications. You can also use other means to develop textual asynchronous conversations, ranging from older technologies, such as email or listservs, to blogs and wikis. For my dissertation research as a graduate student at Temple University, I observed a teacher who used listservs very successfully in a course to foster and augment student conversations. All of these technologies are easily accessible ways of setting students up for a dialogue with you and with each other.

Textual Synchronous Conversations

Chat is well established and can be used as a way to bring students together to discuss course materials. Many think that in even moderate-sized courses, of fifteen to twenty students, chat can be difficult to run if you want everyone to participate. Bender recommends that the number of participants in a synchronous conversation be no more than five (128). In *Preparing Educators for Online Writing Instruction*, Beth Hewett and Christa Ehmann stated that this environment "can be tricky in that it requires highly developed verbal teaching skills and vocabulary" (116). This trickiness is compounded by the fact that many students possess a lingo and fluency in chat that could be confusing and even intimidating to an instructor.

Students spend more and more time having coded conversations using portable devices like phones and technologies like **Twitter**. You might find ways to facilitate conversations in these stripped-down character environments. Cell phones, which are becoming ubiquitous for the twenty-first century college student, pose some interesting educational opportunities. Perhaps we could use them to enhance our students' experiences in our online classes, better employing m-learning, or mobile learning, into our course design (Upadhyay 33). Or perhaps we could frame assignments around students' texting behaviors, having them create a meaningful, complex message in only 140 characters or so. I have followed listserv conversations that describe these types of assignments.

Nontextual Conversations

Because I am privileging writing in my teaching approach, I am focusing on writing technologies, but new tools are emerging and others are improving that allow you to speak to your students or gather them in some virtual way. You can use one of the many technologies that link participants as in a conference call. You can use video technologies to link students via computers and webcams. A quick Web search reveals dozens of options.

Having Students Work in Groups

Often in my efforts to train faculty to teach in the online environment, some people will express concern about the use of groups. Truth be told, group assignments in fully online classes can go awry, as students may disappear or slack off, perhaps more easily than in the onsite environment. Still, if you are a follower of Bruffee, whose groundbreaking article "Collaborative Learning and the 'Conversations of Mankind'" emphasizes the collaborative nature of knowledge construction, you shouldn't feel you must abandon these efforts in your OWcourse. You can use electronic tools to create student peer review groups (Figure 4.2). You can engage in full-blown group projects, as any CMS likely has group functions that create virtual spaces and communication tools. You can also view the entire asynchronous environment as an ongoing collaborative project in the OWcourse. We'll look more at this in Chapter 14.

Engaging Students in a Workshop-Style or Hands-On Activity

The classroom space, especially the writing classroom space, can be a place where students work, writing with the guidance of their instructor and the support of their peers. You can create a similar experience using both asynchronous tools and synchronous chat or **whiteboard** technologies. You can also use slightly more sophisticated networking tools to conduct virtual classrooms where you can visit students' screens, guiding them through a written project. As you know by now, my approach to the OWcourse features far more asynchronous interaction, but the tools exist to recreate workshop environments. This approach

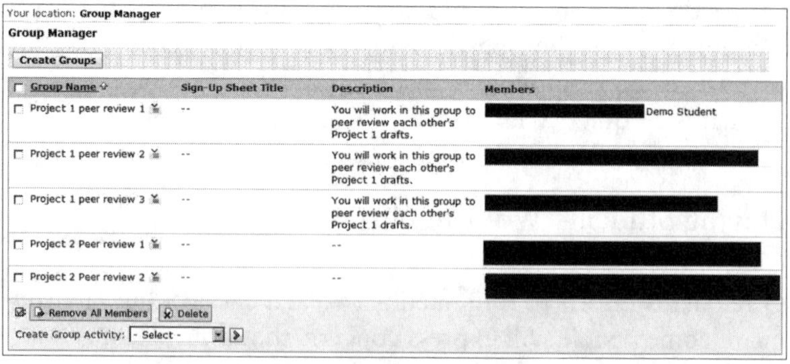

FIGURE 4.2. *Example of how electronic peer review groups look.*

would replicate the type of writing studio "where activities of production are undertaken individually but in a place where others are working and discussing their work simultaneously" (Grego and Thompson 7).

Games and Simulations

Increasingly, teachers are expressing interest in using game-like environments for learning. Conrad and Donaldson have observed that by engaging online students in games and simulations, "real-life skills can be enhanced and learning can be made fun" (93). Video games have been played in networked, real-time environments for years; in an address at Drexel's eLearning 2.0 Conference, Mark Milliron made a distinct point of the potential educational and social value of the gaming environment. Part of our class "workshop" could involve, at some point, offering and perhaps taking part in these kinds of games with our students.

Asking Students to Engage in Unsupervised Work Outside the Classroom

You can ask your online students to engage in out-of-class service or cooperative learning just as readily as you would your onsite students. The only constraint might be that if they live far away, you would have a more difficult time partnering in the creation of out-of-class activities. Still, assignments that involve service learning can be a part of your instruction. According to Conrad and Donaldson, the main characteristic of an authentic activity "is that it simulates an actual situation." They also point out that authentic activities provide that very composition-like opportunity for students to take "meaningful and creative chances" in terms of risk and failure (85). All of this can be maintained in the OWcourse.

The core point is that all of the various ways you might teach your onsite class can be recreated in the OWcourse, some of them more effectively, some less. As I mentioned in the Introduction, you should return to these basic questions: What do you like to do in the classroom? How do you like to teach? If you want to talk to your students about specific material this week, you can work on that. If you want to engage them in an interactive conversation, you can do that. If you want them to create a collaborative project, that can be done as well. Fortunately, many composition instructors teach in student-centered fashion, seeking to build conversation rather than constructing one-way exchanges in which teachers, as Paulo Freire said of his *banking concept* of education, pour information into students, seeing them merely as "receptacles" that need to be filled (58). This approach gives us the opportunity to try some especially innovative things in the online environment, capitalizing on the fact that nearly all student interactions can (although they do not have to) take place in a written way.

One final point at the end of a chapter ostensibly about content, but actually about teaching modalities: the materials you generate to deliver content to your students should be created and stored in such a way that you can conveniently access and reuse them. "There is a tremendous advantage to placing teaching materials into usable enduring materials" (Smith 15). In short, save everything. Consider, though, that if you create materials for exclusive use with a certain CMS, you might find it difficult and annoying to have to recreate them for another system. Ko and Rossen have suggested that you save all your content locally on your own computer, and that if you have the opportunity, you should try out these learning objects in different systems to see what works best (63). We'll explore this idea further in Chapter 16, where I discuss the use of teaching circles and look at other ways of leveraging the technology.

> **Guideline 11**: Various technological tools are available to help you deliver your course content and conduct your class in any style you like; and plenty of resources, including on the Web, in the help section of your CMS, and at the back of this book, exist to assist you.

Pre-term Questions

♦ *What things do you teach that could be defined as "lessons"? What are the main teaching strategies that you employ in the classroom?* Ask yourself questions about that material, its importance to your class, and how you deliver it. Much of online teaching, especially initially, can be envisioned as a migration or transference of your best teaching practices and strategies.

♦ *Do you understand how basic content functions of your CMS work?* How, for instance, do you upload a file of PowerPoint slides?

♦ *How might you want to access these materials in the future?* You'll make your life much easier if you begin online teaching (or any teaching) by grouping useful materials into an organization system that works for you. This is not just a matter of personal convenience. By using electronic tools intelligently, you can look past the simple and spend your precious teacher preparation time innovating and thinking of big-picture problems that you want to solve in your courses.

CHAPTER FIVE

The Writing Course Syllabus: What's Different in Online Instruction?

The OWcourse syllabus needs a greater level of detail than does that of an onsite class. This chapter provides guidance in creating a syllabus, addressing such issues as student participation, grading, course policies and requirements, and instructor availability.

The course syllabus is an important document, regardless of teaching modality. A syllabus "helps students discover at the outset what is expected of them and gives them the security of knowing where they are going" (McKeachie 17). For many instructors, the syllabus has become more than simply a list of readings and due dates, and instead is a contract between teacher and students (Eberly, Newton, and Wiggins). Many teachers are turning to elaborate, detailed syllabi that provide not only the readings, course contact information, and a list of class activities, but also the guidelines for expected class behaviors, department policies, and contact information for campus support services. This approach to the syllabus makes sense in onsite teaching environments, and it might be even more important in the **OW-course**. Although there are many ways to communicate your class expectations to students in an online environment, written text will still likely be of primary importance in their understanding of what your course is about, how they will be evaluated, and what your expectations are for them. Remember that your syllabus is the "initial communication tool that students receive as well as being the most formal mechanism for sharing information with students" (Eberly, Newton, and Wiggins, par. 1). Thus, you'll want to spend time thinking over what you say and *how* you say it in the syllabus.

As with many of the general teaching strategies discussed in this book, plenty of good resources about syllabus creation exist to help in your general thinking about how to build a better syllabus (see Chapter 18). Following are some things you will want especially to consider in developing your syllabus for an OWcourse.

Course Information

You may normally be a little loose in heading your syllabus, calling a class *Writing 101*, for instance. But remember, online students often must choose their courses from a list based upon the numbering and nomenclature of the course. You should provide the *exact* course title on your syllabus, no matter how unwieldy. You also need to provide all relevant course numbers, including section and any identifying number from the university course bulletin or schedule guide. This will help you too, as you might have to choose the online home of your course from a list in your **CMS** that differentiates each course by a term and course number. Remember that if you post the syllabus on a course website, students might access it before they have received contextualizing information from you, so they need to be in the right place.

Your Information

In an onsite class, the assumption is that students know exactly where you will be two or three times a week: inside the classroom designated for that course. Instructors might be less specific regarding other modes of contact in the onsite teaching environment. Online, though, you must determine how you want students to contact you. Some of this might appear obvious, but these decisions have implications for you and your students:

- ◆ **Office**. If your students are not true distance learners, you might be able to meet them in your office. Although exact office hours can seem like a formality that teachers list merely because their departments require it, office hours for an online course should be followed closely. After all, even students who live nearby must make an extra trip to see you. Simply choose times when you will be there.

- ◆ **Email**. Email may be a primary mode of communication, but consider a few things:

  - • **Your account**. Do you want students to use your general account? Or do you want to set up a special email specifically for teaching? Do you have an email through the institution, or do you prefer to use another address? (Note that you can normally forward mail from one account to another, so you might choose to have a teaching alias that funnels all mail to the same account.)

  - • **Accessibility**. I've found that students and I are on different schedules. Occasionally, a student will email me in the wee hours—sometimes I think they can't imagine that I sleep during the term—and seem eager for an immediate response. You might want to designate times each week when you will check and quickly respond to email, and other times when students should expect a lag.

  - • **Internal or external mail**. Most likely, your CMS will have internal email. I seldom use these email functions, but some instructors consider them the best, most efficient way to organize communications in a course. If you use your CMS's internal email system, the advantage is that all messages for your course are there. The downside: this is yet another place to check regularly for electronic communications.

  - • **Message rules**. Especially if you are teaching several sections, you may want to ask students to use an identifier in the subject line. For instance, every student in one class could use the subject line *English 101:856* and all messages from that class would go into the same folder. You could make the rules even more explicit: *English 101:856 Peer Review*. Setting up message rules is simple and worth your time in most email programs, and it can be an effective way to help you stay organized. (In Microsoft Outlook, this function can be found under Tools.)

- ◆ **Phone**. If you list a phone number, make sure you clarify when you can receive course-related calls, and use your local time zone when communicating these times to students who live far away. Remember, if you have a personal cell phone and list that number, you could receive student phone calls at any time.

◆ **Chat, IM, and other modes of synchronous contact.** Normally, you can set up chat spaces through any CMS, or you can use one of myriad other chat programs on the Web. Do you want your students to include you on a buddy list so they know when you are online? Do you want to designate some time each week when you are available within the CMS for chats? I don't keep regular chat hours, but I often open a chat room within my CMS the day before a major writing project is due. I monitor the chat space, hoping to answer last-minute questions.

The more ways your students can contact you, the better; but remember that online, it's easy for students to expect you to be always "on." A critique of online teaching that I sometimes hear is that teachers feel as if they are expected to be perpetually connected. You can establish reasonable guidelines for this connectivity the first time you teach if you clarify them in the syllabus.

> **Guideline 12**: Make sure that your electronic self's availability is in accord with the schedule your atom self wants to keep.

Texts

One of the first sections of most syllabi describes the course texts. Especially if you teach required classes in large composition programs, the texts are often ordered for you, so you don't have to order them yourself. However, remember in distance learning that your students might not have access to the campus bookstore. They need complete and precise ordering information, including the ISBN and edition number. If you want students to purchase a particular version or edition, identify that clearly. The beginning of your course can be hampered considerably if students have trouble accessing or acquiring the texts because the syllabus wasn't clear.

Follow similar thinking with any e-texts you assign. Make sure they are not on websites that block student access for any reason. Work out these problems beforehand, because many students will not discover until the night before the term starts—when it's too late—that they don't have the text or can't access the readings.

Course Description

Especially if you are teaching a class that you have taught **f2f** before, you'll want to think through the course description carefully. You will achieve the same core outcomes (that similarity is a foundational concept in this book) in your online writing class as in your onsite courses, but a moment of reflection will be helpful. Remember, this course probably will have a much heavier component of writing than did your onsite courses. Is that something you should explain in your course description? Have someone else read the description, because students might only encounter the description as text with no qualifying or clarifying information from you.

Course Policies

This section of the syllabus should undergo significant change when you migrate online. Course policies will be different because the students' experience will be different.

Rules of an Online Class

One major change you might introduce with your online class is a more explicit set of rules. Students might refer to their online syllabi more frequently than they did their onsite course syllabi, and they might need guidelines to understand course expectations and the course culture you will establish. Provide detail: describe how e-conversations should take place (see Chapter 8), when they should complete the readings, how they should contact you, and so on.

Accountability

In my syllabus I now include language to inform students of their increased accountability in an OWcourse. I make it clear that they are responsible to help build the knowledge of the course. They must be active learners. To help them understand what this means, you might include a link to a learning style survey (there are many: type *learning style survey* into a search engine). Part of their accountability, I tell students, begins with a close reading of the course documents, starting with the syllabus and regularly checking the course homepage. They are also accountable in completing their assignments and in their treatment of me and their classmates. I have always felt that I work hard for my students; this category of accountability is designed so we all understand that it takes a partnership to succeed in an OWcourse.

Disabilities

Students with disabilities might have a different set of rights in online courses. You'll want to provide a clear way for them to contact your local office of disability services. Remember, some of these students will not be on campus.

Escape Clauses

Let students know how to drop your class and how long they are allowed to do so without penalty. Link to the academic calendar and to your institution's academic policies, and make sure that students understand the drop/add rules.

Document Conventions

An OWcourse is about a regular exchange of documents. If you are particular about the type of electronic documents you want to receive—and I suggest that you be specific—you should list those rules in the syllabus. You will also want students to name their files usefully (see Chapter 6 for more on organization). List this information, perhaps with some naming examples. In my classes I want students to name their document files so I can easily identify and organize them, so I use the example of *Scott WProject1f08.doc*.

Rules for Incomplete or Late Assignments

If you have rules for late or missed work, make them clear. You might create even more detailed rules, perhaps describing exactly how many hours constitute a certain grade deduction. If students cannot pass the course unless they complete all assignments, make sure they understand that in the syllabus. Remember, this is a contract, and as long as you have laid out an explicit set of rules, you have covered yourself—and helped prepare students for the work ahead.

Skill Sets

Are there any particular skill sets that your students might need to perform well in your course? Are there expectations that they know how to engage in a particular level of research? That they can operate or possess a certain software? Or that they know how to use your university's library? If so, you can list these expectations in the syllabus, including any links that might help them.

Technology

This is a key category in your OWcourse policies. You should make explicit what you expect of students. Don't hold back, because you're not doing students a favor by downplaying what they will need in terms of technology. If they will need to access your CMS four times a week and be able to download large files, the student who can use only a public-access computer with a slow connection a few times a week should know this up front. Are there particular file formats you will use? Do you have specific rules for the old "computer ate my homework" excuse? Tech problems are inevitable, so think about this: what will you accept as a reason for a delayed assignment? You have described when you will access your email, but how about your students? Do you have expectations about when they will be online? You might use this section of the syllabus to clearly state how often students should expect to be online, and specify their ability to *access* a computer. This might seem obvious, but not all students—and not all students who want to take an online course—have easy access to a computer. I use strong language to discourage students from taking the class if they don't have regular computer access, because I don't want them to set themselves up for failure.

Schedule

I use a **Weekly Plan** approach to organize my courses (see Chapter 6). One myth about teaching online is that you must have everything scheduled and ready to go far in advance of the start of the term. In both onsite and online teaching, although you certainly need a clear sense of the overall expectations and the map of the course, you shouldn't feel that you need to frame out every moment of activity before term begins. For some instructors, this kind of front-end control is necessary. If so, that's fine. But others, and I am one of them, like the flexibility of being able to shift the course content and pace as the term proceeds. You can do that in an online course with no detriment to your students. Nevertheless, you need to provide some type of schedule in the syllabus. At the minimum, you should include this information:

- **Major due dates.** List the dates (or even just the weeks) when drafts are due.

- **Scheduled exams.**

- **Weekly deadlines that are unchanging.** If your message board posts are always due on Wednesdays at 6 p.m., for instance, you should note that. If you always make a quiz based on the readings available on Tuesday from 9 a.m. to 5 p.m., indicate that.

- **Special events taking place during the term.**

Preparing Students for the OWcourse

A final component of your syllabus should be a statement—which you could include as a separate file—that describes for your students how their participation in this course might be different because it is an OWcourse. Some students will never have taken an online course, and a reassuring statement on the syllabus will help orient them to what they can expect in this environment. In the Teaching Materials Appendix, I provide the wording I used in one course, and you'll note how it reinforces the material described above.

Make It a Contract

I add one final piece to my syllabus. As I have mentioned, I view the syllabus as a contract. I require at the beginning of my course—every course, not just OWcourses—that the students email me indicating that they have read carefully the policies of the course and that they agree with them. Although not legally binding, this allows me to curtail student objections to matters in the syllabus, as I make it clear that they have indicated their agreement with the course and its objectives. That sets a tone I try to develop all term: we are working together in a partnership of mutual understanding.

Guideline 13: Your OWcourse syllabus should provide more detail than other syllabi you have used. This will be the primary document that describes the course, and you should view it as a detailed contract of the working relationship you will build with your students.

Pre-term Questions

- *How early can you begin working on a draft of your syllabus?* The syllabus is a great document to percolate a bit in your brain, so getting an early start is important.

- *What resources can you draw on to develop your syllabus?* Don't be shy about incorporating template materials from your program or from other resources.

◆ *When are you realistically available, and when and how students should contact you?* This will help you determine exactly what kind of presence you will be for your students.

◆ *Are the objectives and description of the course clear?* What is apparent in an onsite course might be less clear in the online environment. Remove any guesswork by laying out clearly to your students what you expect of them.

◆ *Who can read your syllabus for you before you hand it out?* Find a colleague and swap syllabi. Is the "contract" aspect clear? If not, what can you do to make this more explicit? Would the document be clear to someone who has not spoken to you?

CHAPTER SIX

Organization: Redundancy, and Helping Students—and You— Keep Things Straight

Staying organized in your OWcourse can be difficult. We'll look at some simple ways to organize the course materials, and I'll offer some tips for dealing with the inevitable crush of information—emails, electronic files, and so on—that accompanies teaching in an online environment.

Thinking about our information-based culture, I wonder if the rewards go not to the smartest or even hardest working, but instead to the best organized. As C. William Pollard said, "Information is a source of learning. But unless it is organized, processed, and available to the right people in a format for decision making, it is a burden, not a benefit" (123). In *The Cult of Information*, Theodore Roszak noted, "If anything, we suffer from a glut of unrefined, undigested information flowing in from every medium around us" (162). You might be skilled at keeping your stream of incoming digital information in order and accessible, but you might be surprised by the level of organization needed to keep your **OWcourse** running smoothly. And you'll want to be prepared. As Barber remarked, "A basic strategy for teachers moving into the online classroom is to plan ahead" (255).

Remember, when teaching writing online, many of your classroom interactions will be in writing through media like message boards, email, and chats. You'll need to come up with ways to organize and present course materials, especially in terms of the course schedule. You'll need smart, simple organizational methods to keep class communications straight. And, as Smith pointed out in her book multiple times, your organization must remain consistent across the various learning objects in your course. Patti Wolf agreed. "Be consistent in the conventions you use" in your course (par. 1). Think about the course as a whole, and plan to keep the presentation, style, placement, and format of your materials consistent.

Organization for its own sake is valuable in teaching but hardly seems worthy of a chapter. Numerous readings can help you organize your work better; type *organize computer files* into a search engine, and you'll get more than one million hits. My particular point about organization in an OWcourse is that some advantages of teaching online will be lost if you are disorganized, because you won't be able to draw easily on one of the most powerful resources in the technology-mediated writing course: students' day-to-day, **informal writing**, which you can use to help build their skills. So although being organized is always advantageous in terms of teaching quality, online you can teach more effectively if you can easily draw on the material that your students are creating as part of their regular work in the class.

In an online writing class, unlike in an onsite class, you don't have as much control over when communication occurs and flows to you, as students can contact you any time and are often working around the clock. Of course this flexibility is one of the key advantages of online learning for everyone, but you can quickly find yourself behind when you realize that you are receiving lots of messages but don't have a good way to save them, or, more important, you can't find them later when you need them. A number of technology tools can help you find files and other data (James Fallows reviews several tools in a 2006 *Atlantic Monthly* article), so it's a matter of trying to find a way to put these tools to work for you.

> **Guideline 14:** Don't underestimate the importance of being organized in the online teaching environment. Before you teach online for the first time, make sure your files and folder systems reflect the kind of structure you want for the class and allow you to use student texts to good advantage throughout the course.

By *organization,* I mean not just your ability to keep things straight for yourself, but also your ability to present course materials so students can find things easily and intuitively. At the high end of such approaches, we move into sophisticated course design; but for most of us, being consistent, clear, and simple using a **CMS** will go a long way toward helping students navigate the course easily. Consider starting off the term with a kind of CMS scavenger hunt, asking students to roam around the site and find different documents or functions.

Email

Does your inbox contain thousands of messages? I'm surprised at how many people I run into who don't have even a basic email folder system. If you dump all your emails from the class into one folder (or let them languish in your inbox), you not only will lose some of the advantages of using student writing, but you will go mad trying to find old messages, which might be important as they constitute a record of interaction between you and your students.

Email folders don't cost you anything, so don't skimp on them. Create many subfolders, broken down as specifically as possible into particular assignments, peer reviews, grade inquiries, sent messages, and other topics. You'll want a folder for general conversations you have with students. I always create a folder called *Woes,* which is my catchall for problems, tech-related and otherwise, that occur during the term. If you teach multiple sections online, think even more about how to organize the inevitable pile of messages. Most email programs have ways—often called *rules*—of organizing messages automatically based on the sender's name, sender's email, subject, and so on. Ask your students to use a subject line with the same identifying phrase, such as *Section 7,* in any message they send to you , so those messages automatically go to a predetermined folder (see Chapter 5 for more on this topic).

You also will want to create a structure for responding to messages. Part of your organization in online instruction involves smart prioritizing of responsibilities. If you don't use message rules, your students' emails will be mixed in with the rest of your daily email flow. Smith has noted that as she became experienced teaching online, "I learned to prioritize the order in which I will answer messages from students" (86). You'll need to find ways to determine when you must respond immediately to a student and when you can wait. Ask students to help with this by being judicious about when they send emails and by entering useful subject lines (the subject *English* is not much help to you when looking at fifty emails).

Message Boards

Before the term begins, spend time learning the organization of the message board you will use, and take advantage of its organization functions: indenting, bolding of new messages, subject naming, and alternate views (by subject or date, for instance) (Figure 6.1). You also will want to create easy-to-remember naming conventions for **thread**s (Figure 6.2). In week one, inform students how the threads work, so they can keep the conversation flowing. And this might seem picayune, but remember that message boards

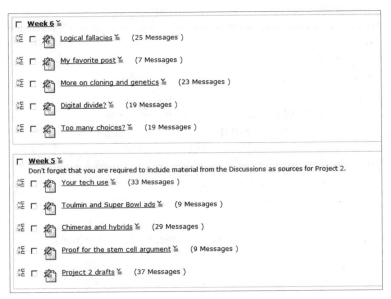

Figure **6.1.** *Message board topics organized by week on Bb Vista Discussions.*

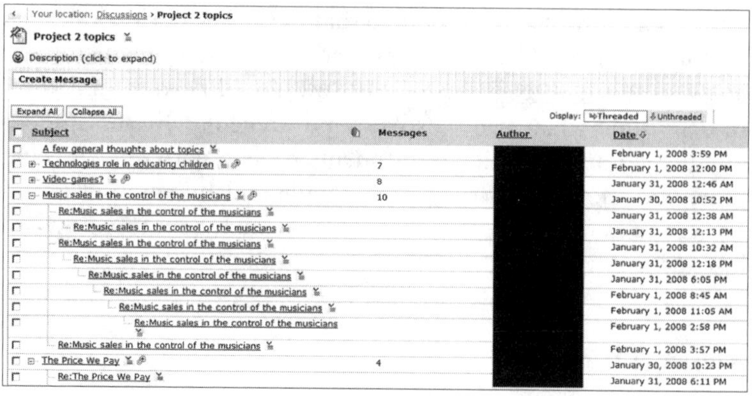

FIGURE 6.2. *Threaded message board conversation on Bb Vista Discussions.*

might have different views: if there are lots of messages, students might have to click on an icon to see a second or third message page. I spend much more time on message boards in Chapter 8.

File Naming

Your course will generate a number of files, many of them text based, and you will want a good folder system similar to one you create for email (perhaps with the same titles, to keep things straight). Again, use lots of detail, and let your subfolder system go as deep as needed. For instance, although it's a good idea to call a folder *Drafts* and then save all drafts in it, you should probably further subdivide into folders for specific assignments.

As I mentioned in Chapter 5, you should give students specific rules for naming files. If you don't, when you receive your students' first projects, 75 percent will be named *Project 1*. Ask students to use a simple file-naming convention like first name, last initial, and assignment: *ScottWProject1f08.doc*.

An Additional Word on File-Naming Conventions

The same naming conventions you require of students should become part of your standard practice. This might seem basic and obvious, but in general, people don't organize their files for maximum benefit. Fallows said that "the attempt to create effective data-management programs" is one of the "software world's longest-running . . . sagas" (140). Now, the pressure to have complex file structures might be lessened with the refinement of desktop search tools, but you'll find that in your online class creation efforts, you will create and receive an enormous number of files. It can be overwhelming.

Remember to name files for a class in a uniform, easily identifiable way. Each file should have a phrase or *slug* that identifies when it was created. So my syllabus for my fall English 101 course might look like this: 08fallEng101syllabus. There's no need to be stingy in your naming practices: it's better to create names that actually mean something to you later when you are looking for a file than to create a highly arcane code system that you can't sort out. And your system should be easy enough to remember that you can re-create it.

Guideline 15: Make sure your syllabus has clear file-naming conventions for your students, as you will receive many files from them, and you'll want a smart method of organizing these files. Make sure you follow similar conventions in the files that you yourself create for any class.

Using the system above, when I file that file, it will always have the same extension, telling me when I created it. Other advantages in managing files include using headers and footers and placing useful **metadata** within the files themselves.

Without question, you will refine your organizational approach every time you teach, so don't lock yourself into a rigid system. Pick what works for you, realizing that organization is often very individualistic. As computer scientist Roger Schank noted, "Memory is highly idiosyncratic. One person's organization is not another's" (267). Regardless of your organization system, spending a few minutes pre-term thinking about information flow will save you time and reduce your stress, possibly helping you be a better teacher.

Links and Multimedia

In addition to all the files and messages you will receive, as you expand your use of online tools, you will also have an ever-expanding list of links and multimedia materials for your classes. Again, spend some time before you start the term thinking about how to organize that material, even if you haven't begun to assemble it. You can use your browser's bookmark function as a rudimentary way to organize links, but bookmark organizing software like **delicious** increases the usefulness of such a process exponentially. Programs such as Google Desktop or Microsoft OneNote can help you organize and access various files, links, and other resources. In fact, the growing sophistication of these search/organization programs suggests that users will soon be able to organize *after* the fact: you can easily find anything via word-string searches, so you can put files anywhere because you can recall them in a search engine-like way. (For instance, I got a lot of mileage out of Google Desktop as I prepared the manuscript of this book.) But you could easily end the term with links, video, and audio spread throughout your message boards, email, and CMS pages. Compiling all that material will be a nuisance, and of course it will lose its value as a teaching/learning tool if you can't find something. One of the advantages of teaching online is that you can leverage digital reproducibility through course modules and so forth, but this advantage is lost if you don't have ways to organize and then retrieve data.

The Weekly Plan: Keeping Students Organized

One of my key methods of helping students—and myself—stay organized in my OWcourses is the **Weekly Plan**. This simple, yet elegant solution to course organization allows me to provide my students each week with a complete set of the activities they must accomplish, broken down into specific (and thus easily completed) tasks. The Plan—I use capitals to reinforce for students its hallowed stature in the course—is easy to create using an HTML or Word table. To produce a slightly heightened visual effect, I use a bicolored table with simple, straightforward column categories addressed to the students: What do I do? What are the specific instructions? Where do I find the work or the assignment? When is it due?

In the Teaching Materials Appendix is a sample Weekly Plan from one of my courses. Simple in concept, the Weekly Plan is a key way I practice useful *redundancy* in communicating with my students. Each week, I can put all the various instructions and guidelines in one place. This solves many subtle but nettlesome problems encountered in an OWcourse, where students might be working in several different environments and will have different sets of instructions for each environment.

> **Guideline 16**: A simple organization plan for students, such as a Weekly Plan, can go a long way toward helping them stay on track in the course.

Multiple Computers

How do you keep organized if you have more than one computer? I encountered this problem when I first starting teaching, and I approached it in a wrong-headed way: I thought there must be some mystery solution that eluded me. After talking to people whose lives revolved around technology, I learned that anyone who uses multiple machines struggles with this issue. I mention it here in case you have a different computer at one or more sites, and you are teaching online.

The problem might be most easily solved by having a laptop—or, increasingly, a powerful phone or **PDA**—with you at all times. If not, you'll need a way to keep files and other information synched between devices. Many PDA programs can do this, or you could use an external hard drive. In the electronic realm of **Web 2.0**, the answer now appears to be cheap online storage that is accessible anywhere. Tools like Google Docs or Dropbox (which National Council of Teachers of English [NCTE] blogger Traci Gardner reviewed positively) allow you to store files and retrieve them from any computer with Internet access. You could also rely on tools like VPN (virtual private network) to keep your email and other files synched, regardless of where you work.

As with many topics I discuss in this book, these solutions are far more on the tech side than our conversation allows. You can find solutions through online searches, but perhaps it's best to draw on your local IT department for help.

A Word on Redundancy

In *Cybernetics*, Norbert Wiener wrote, "We can hardly expect that any important message is entrusted for transmission to a single neuron, nor that any important operation is entrusted to a single neuronal mechanism" (144). When teaching writing online, simply put, we should provide information to our students through multiple means. *Redundancy* and *repetition* will help students stay on track so we can focus on the more challenging and complex task of helping them improve their writing. Our organizational methods should have redundancy built in and should provide students with instructions that create useful categories, or **chunking**: Smith explained that "chunking is grouping pieces of information into meaningful segments," and she also pointed out that repetition is key online (64).

> **Guideline 17**: Redundancy is crucial when you deliver information in your OWcourses.

In my OWcourses, redundancy is built into my course organization. I try to send the same message to students several different ways. I don't want to nag them, but I want them to stay on top of their assignments. I think that confidence, and a sense of orientation, helps by allowing them to focus on improving their writing. So for instance, if they have a final draft of a writing project due, they might receive this information in several ways:

- The due date is on the syllabus they receive at the start of the class (and to which there is always a link on the homepage).

- The due date is listed on the specific instructions for that writing project, which I provide separately when I assign the project.

- Each week, I provide students with the Weekly Plan that lists all activities, including the due date for the project.

- In my comments reviewing the rough draft, I mention—either in writing or via AV comments—when the final draft is due.

- The course announcements on the homepage include a note about the due date. I also include a "pop-up" reminder that appears when they first log in.

- A group email from me, often sent a day or two before the deadline, reminds them of the due date.

Some of this might look like overkill, and I don't use all these methods with every assignment, but scheduling reminders are often embedded in course documents. In fact, only the email and pop-up option are "intrusive"—not really the right term, considering that I'm trying to help them do their best in the course.

The key is to reinforce your message about assignments, expectations, and requirements in several ways. Although this is good teaching practice in general, it's even more important in the OWcourse, where it is your responsibility to help students stay on schedule. This advice is in line with Wiener's quoting of Lewis Carroll's principle in *The Hunting of the Snark*: "What I tell you three times is true" (145).

Pre-term Questions

- *How can you optimize the organizational structure of your files, emails, and other components of your course before the term begins?*

- *Are programs available to help you organize the inevitable information flow?* There are many. Spending just half an hour seeing what works for you could save you an enormous amount of time later.

- *Have you identified clear file-naming conventions in your syllabus?* A simple line or two will help many students remember what you require.

- *Are you prepared for a lot of emails and other information?* The first week will probably be the toughest, as you grow accustomed to how much access students have to you in this environment.

- *Do your course documents provide information to students in multiple ways?*

CHAPTER SEVEN

Readings: Lots of Online Options, But the Book Is Not Dead!

Writing, of course, is closely linked with reading. This chapter examines ways to assign readings, to ensure that students read, and to approach reading in the OWcourse.

The debate about reading online versus traditional reading of print materials, especially for our students' generation, has accelerated recently. Studies show that students do much less "traditional" reading than they once did. According to a *New York Times* article,

> Last fall the National Endowment for the Arts issued a sobering report linking flat or declining national reading test scores among teenagers with the slump in the proportion of adolescents who said they read for fun.
>
> According to Department of Education data cited in the report, just over a fifth of 17-year-olds said they read almost every day for fun in 2004, down from nearly a third in 1984. Nineteen percent of 17-year-olds said they never or hardly ever read for fun in 2004, up from 9 percent in 1984. (Rich, pars. 15–16)

Of course, what students should read in a first-year writing course has long been debated anyway by compositionists, who favor various viewpoints on the appropriateness of different readings. (Perhaps one result of this debate has been the recent emergence of a *writing studies* approach, in which the core reading and study content of the course is material about writing and rhetoric [Downs and Wardle].) To further complicate—or simplify—matters, the slowly growing popularity of electronic devices for reading e-books (Stone and Rich) may provide teachers with alternative ways of providing readings for their classes.

Whether you teach online or onsite, many questions about which reading to choose may remain the same, but as with other aspects of your teaching, the **OWcourse** may lead you to rethink your use of readings in composition courses.

The Book

In a discussion of Web versus print-based reading on the Writing Program Administrator's **listserv**, Nick Carbone said,

> When you walk across a college campus—and I walk across about 20 per year, all over the country—you always still see students sitting in chairs, under trees, in the library, in class-rooms, and in the student center using books, using paper. Reading, talking, note-taking by hand, picking up course packs, and so on. (par. 5)

The death of the book, to borrow an aphorism, might be greatly exaggerated. First of all, if you like using an anthology in your **FYW** courses and want to continue this in your OWcourses, then do so. After all, reading is part of the *homework* of your course. Students read for their courses on their own time; nothing about that needs to change in the online setting. You can provide students with the same types of readings and assign the same relative work load and schedule. The students will, as they have always done, read this material as part of the homework of the course; you then have options to engage them in conversations about these readings that will help them develop their written projects.

In using a book, then, not much has to be different, but if you are teaching in a genuine distance situation, you'll want to consider the logistics of your choice: primarily, to think about the accessibility of the texts you choose. Many of us are accustomed to having a centralized place—like the bookstore—where students can purchase their course texts. This will not apply to your students if they live outside a reasonable driving distance from campus. Mainly, you will want to plan earlier about making texts available. A cautionary note: **CMS** systems sometimes do not allow student access until right before the term starts. You can either request earlier access or contact students, perhaps through email, ahead of time to let them know which texts they are expected to have when the term starts.

Guideline 18: It's fine to use your regular course books in your OWcourse, but make sure you provide students with a way to access those books *before* the class begins.

When thinking about your readings, remember another advantage of using a course textbook: publishers have become increasingly savvy about creating quality e-learning materials that can be bundled with a textbook. Some of these offerings are impressive and comprehensive. Spend a few hours investigating these materials, and you'll find a great mix of texts, **multimodal** materials, and assignments. Many of these materials can be loaded into your CMS with minimal trouble.

The Open Web

In online teaching, you might naturally be drawn to the many texts available on the Web. Indeed, you can put together many substantive reading lists simply from free, openly available materials that anyone can use without fear of copyright violation (see Chapter 15 about copyright). Many FYW modules, and even whole courses, are geared toward a current theme; quick searches reveal hundreds of thousands of articles, videos, and images for students to read.

Your challenge will be to maintain an organized way of delivering these materials (see Chapter 6). In fact, when you start to assemble your own reading packets and lists online, you might reflect on how much we take the humble book for granted; it's a fascinating technology, especially in terms of organization (see Ong 130–36). Fortunately, a CMS can help us stay organized.

You can provide a page on your CMS with links and descriptors that include dates and other information about the readings.

You could even bundle readings with other materials, such as the assignments that accompany those readings, into modules like **SCORM** or into a media library. When gathering reading materials, you will have to make certain choices:

♦ Do you want to show all of the readings in the beginning of the term, or do you want to keep some hidden (or even upload them later)?

♦ Do you want to use a table of contents in the course, or will you lead students to the readings in weekly instructions and/or the syllabus?

♦ Will you provide brief annotations of the materials that you supply?

♦ Do you want to simply provide a link, or do you want a file format such as Word, **rich text**, or **PDF**?

♦ Are the links you provide *durable*, that is, will they change? At times, you will use material that for some reason—perhaps because of copyright violation—is taken down from the Web. For instance, some YouTube materials are continually removed, probably due to copyright issues, only to emerge again with a new link.

Many magazines and newspapers have comprehensive websites, not to mention the seemingly endless number of **blog**s and **wiki**s that focus on specific topics of interest. If you are seeking material specifically about writing, you'll find many resources. If you want to discuss comma splices, for instance, Google reveals more than 90,000 sites in response to the search term *comma splice*.

Guideline 19: You'll find millions of Web readings and multimedia materials to use in your class. Before the term begins, think through your course texts and spend some time—it needn't be a lot—finding Web readings and organizing them on your CMS for your students.

The Library

Our students aren't the only ones who overlook the library as a resource. Libraries have access to vast electronic holdings, and I have yet to meet a librarian who didn't eagerly assist me in developing a set of readings for a course. Librarians not only will help you access articles but are knowledgeable about copyright and can help you better organize materials for a class. You could approach the use of the library in several ways:

- ◆ Provide students with citations for articles they need to find and read for your class. Thus, part of their learning in the course is navigating the library's databases to find these articles for themselves.

- ◆ Work with your library to develop a course pack specific to your needs. Aside from the organizational benefits to students when you present such a pack in your CMS, you will have received the library's support in terms of the sticky topic of copyright (see Chapter 15). And the material will be organized.

- ◆ Ask students to use library resources and databases to find readings specific to their projects rather than sharing a common set of readings. This approach can be especially useful in OWcourses, as students are in the mode of using electronic materials.

Use your library's resources. Library staff at campuses where I have worked have been highly enthusiastic and incredibly creative about developing materials for teaching, yet I think we sometimes overlook them, leaving all that expertise untapped.

Multimodal Texts

Because you are now teaching online, this is not a privileged area, but perhaps the increased awareness of technology that accompanies an OWcourse will lead you to investigate using more multimodal texts in the course. The array of audio and video materials on the Web can be used in conjunction with conventional texts to create a different kind of "reading" experience for students. For some of us, the move to multimodality may come with growing pains, simply because we haven't always been trained to *think* in those terms as teachers; but you can find many usable images, videos, and audio materials for students on almost any topic imaginable.

For example, the Wikipedia assignment I describe in Chapter 9 involves a variety of texts, broadly defined: a cartoon, a video, a magazine article, and a chapter in the students' writing handbook. This was a cool assignment that allowed students to build from a diversity of texts.

Student Texts

As you plan the reading offerings, be aware that your online students will read a lot of their colleagues' writing in the course. This reading material can have a much larger presence in an OWcourse than in an onsite course. A whole host of assignments can stem from students' reading of each other's texts (see Chapter 9). Think about the amount of reading they do in the online environment as you create the course; their everyday interactions are different in this environment, as they are filled with reading and writing about each other's texts. If one of your primary goals as a teacher is to help them refine their reading skills, there may be great opportunities for this in the OWcourse.

How Do We Know They Have Read?

This question is, of course, not just applicable to the online course experience. I have had numerous conversations with colleagues who expressed frustration because in their **f2f** class session, few students had read the required materials. For many classes based around the assumption that students have read the texts, if they *don't* read, the class is flat and unproductive. There are several strategies you might follow in an online class to encourage your students not just to read the texts, but to do so with some level of care and precision.

Give Reading and Studying Advice in the Syllabus

Students might be unaccustomed to the individualized environment of the OWcourse. As I mention in Chapter 8, you can create specific language about reading each other's work. You can also include some language—and links to materials—that will help students understand how to be better students in the online environment: even get down to specifics, such as where and when they will do their reading, particularly for first-year students who might benefit from a conversation about how to study in noisy dorms. All of our students could probably use some good study habit advice, but online students might find it particularly useful. A standard part of my instruction in FYW courses includes a reading workshop, no matter which modality I am using.

Quizzes

Quizzing can be a constructive way to help your students read more closely. Ways of administering these quizzes are described more fully in Chapter 12, and you might look at my article, "Quizzes Boost Comprehension, Confidence," and Brad Thompson's article, "If I Quiz Them, They Will Come." Both articles describe constructive ways to conduct quizzes, and although they are geared toward in-class use of quizzing, the underlying idea is to use quizzes as a positive tool to encourage reading and thus better learning.

In my online classes, every week I give a straightforward five-question quiz based strictly on the readings. I administer the quiz through my CMS. The questions are easy—all I want the students to do is demonstrate that they have read. The quiz is always on the same day of the week, which I believe helps students with the pacing of the course (see Chapter 13). When they open the quiz, they have five minutes to complete it. Because the questions are simple, five minutes is more than enough time. Do students cheat? I am not proctoring the quiz, so of course they may be able to cheat, but I have a few barriers in place. One is simplicity. The quiz is so easy that it would be almost embarrassing for them to cheat on it. Another useful obstacle is the five-minute time limit. Also, each quiz is worth only a small part of the overall course grade. These barriers are designed to make the quiz so easy that it's almost more trouble to cheat than it is to read the material and take the quiz honestly. If you're skeptical, I point out that almost any CMS provides you with the ability to create **question sets** or to randomize the order of questions. Question sets are a group of questions that you create, and then the CMS randomly picks from the set to create the quiz. So students can all have different questions, even if the questions are only slightly different.

Posts and Other Informal Writing

I seem to have less trouble with my online students in terms of reading than I do with my onsite students. This is because of my heavy use of posts and other **informal writing**: *all* students, at multiple points each week, must write about the texts in ways that require close readings. When they don't spend enough time reading, it's often obvious. When you consider that in most onsite classes, even energetic ones, all of the students do not speak in a given class session, you'll see another potential advantage of the OWcourse experience.

Strong Evidence Connections between Readings and Written Projects

You can also encourage students to read in your online class by requiring them to draw on evidence from the course readings for their more extensive written projects. This means they must read posts with an eye toward finding evidence for their own arguments, and this should make them much more diligent readers of the course materials, including their colleagues' posts and other informal writing.

Personal Contact

If you notice that students are not reading—and this may be easier to see in an OWcourse—you can reach out to them personally. Sometimes a word of encouragement from you can help a student connect better with the class and be more assertive in undertaking all of the assignments.

All of the earlier advice is designed to encourage students to read, but there is a point at which they must be responsible for their own work in the course. I think we should help encourage that responsibility, while also expecting students to be accountable for their own learning. That is why I include an entry in the policies section of my syllabus about accountability.

Guideline 20: There are many constructive ways of encouraging your students to read in your OWcourse. Low-stakes response methods will help them demonstrate to you—and each other—that they have read the course texts carefully.

A Word about Copyright

Copyright is well covered in many books and articles about teaching in general and online teaching specifically. Using a variety of means, including file-sharing sites, students can—and often do—download pirated copies of textbooks, and many instructors have reacted to the increasingly high cost of textbooks by using electronic alternatives (Bray). In online teaching, it might make sense, for many reasons, to provide e-texts. But before you use e-texts in your OWcourse, you need to understand how such texts can be distributed and what the implications are if students—or sometimes, the teacher—use them in violation of copyright. This topic is covered in Chapter 15. I will simply say here that you want to consult personnel on your campus, mainly librarians, who are experienced and educated about this issue.

Pre-term Questions

♦ *Will you use a textbook, or can you create class readings from materials on the Web and in your library?* If you have used a textbook as the backbone of your onsite course and you are migrating that course online, you don't need to change that. Images, videos, and online articles can be the core of your course reading or can help support textbook readings. Using these materials is simply a matter of your creativity and willingness to spend time searching for such material.

◆ *If you plan to use a textbook, what e-tools might accompany the book?* Ask someone in your department or a publisher about these tools. Publishers are happy to discuss the tools they feature; sometimes you can have technology packages bundled with a book.

◆ *How can you ensure that all of your students can access the texts* before *the term starts?* In this area, the online class is truly different: your students may not all be able to access the bookstore on campus. Supply them with information about the texts you will use at least a week before the first day of the term.

◆ *How will you organize reading materials on your CMS?* Create a *Readings* folder on your course homepage so you can place relevant readings there. Don't subject your students to a homepage full of scattered links to readings.

◆ *How can you be sure that your students read?* A variety of strategies exist, including the use of reading quizzes and asking students to use parts of each other's posts in their major projects. You can also use the conversation medium of your class to push students to make sure they read.

◆ *Who can you consult about copyright?* See the end of this book for some reading advice about copyright, and also consult your local librarian. (See Chapter 15.)

CHAPTER EIGHT

Conversation: Online, Course "Talk" Can Become Writing

This chapter describes a cornerstone of my online pedagogy: the use of asynchronous message boards to facilitate student communication. I also mention some other technologies that enable students to have a conversation online.

One of my primary pedagogical goals is *conversation*. Online, these conversations can take place much as they would in an onsite class, but they have a significant advantage for the online writing teacher: they are often written. So we don't have to think of our virtual conversations as just as good as our onsite conversations—they can be better. Adult education expert S. Joseph Levine said of online course conversations, "Not seen as merely a tool to make online learning 'as good as' in-person education, the online discussion board presents unique opportunities for teaching in new ways" ("Online" 73). This chapter is about capitalizing on those opportunities.

As I mentioned in the Introduction, we start the migration to online teaching with our pedagogical goals. For me, regardless of whether I am teaching online, **hybrid**, or onsite, I want my students talking to each other because, following from the work of social constructionists like Bruffee, I feel that the dialogue between myself and my students builds the knowledge of my writing courses most effectively. I can't accomplish this by just talking *at* my students. M. M. Bakhtin stated, "To some extent, primacy belongs to the response, as the activating principle: it creates the ground for understanding, it prepares the ground for an active and engaged understanding" (282). In my courses, I want to

- ◆ create an open environment in which students feel free to contribute their ideas;

- ◆ allow all students to voice their thoughts;

- ◆ give students time to think over complex points made by me, and by their colleagues, and respond to those points; and

- ◆ write, write, and write some more.

Asynchronous Conversations through Message Boards

You can have conversations in many ways using digital technology, but I will focus on using **asynchronous** communication via message boards. Message boards can work even more effectively than my best in-class conversations for the earlier objectives; and I should point out, with all humbleness, that I have worked hard on my in-class dialogue facilitation skills, and I receive many compliments on course evaluations from students about the open, friendly environment of my onsite classes. If you haven't used the simple technology of message boards, prepare to be amazed by the kind of work your students can do in this environment. Writing instructors have long been intrigued by e-communication environments. Some years ago Beth Kolko noted that in text-based virtual world environments (sometimes called **MUDs**: multi-user dungeons) words carry the day (62). I have found that the semi-formal writing my students produce on message boards is often astounding, and that message boards can provide a major vehicle for much of what I want to do in an **OWcourse**.

All **CMS** packages have some form of message board, and the boards themselves are versatile and easy to use (many applications are free: type *free message board* into a search engine for lots of options). Although I will stop short—but *just* short—of calling them the holy grail of writing pedagogy, message boards provide a means of facilitating the *efficient* sharing of writing in your class in ways that open up intriguing opportunities for teaching, learning, and writing.

In addition, some normal constraints of **synchronous** or onsite conversations are absent in the message board environment. In synchronous or onsite environments, the conversation is fairly linear, almost always meaning that not everyone can participate. With message boards, conversations can build in parallel fashion. Some students might be shy about speaking their minds in a classroom conversation or even a fast-paced chat setting, where by the time you respond, the rest of the group is on to another topic. The relative anonymity of the message boards can create, as Gail Hawisher said of networked conversations, an open environment with more equitable participation ("Electronic" 88), or what Addesso called a place where "there are no lost opportunities to speak" (114). Lester Faigley took it a step further in his comment about networked classrooms: "The utopian dream of an equitable sharing of classroom authority, at least during the duration of a class discussion, has been achieved" (167). Message boards provide students with reflective time, and many "welcome the opportunity to compose thoughtful, probing contributions" (Collison et al. 2). Hewett and Ehmann noted in tutoring situations "the fact that [online writing instruction] often is anonymous *and* non-real-time gives the student the time to make drafting and revising decisions without the pressure of an immediate audience" (159). I find that the natural delay helps conversations on the boards achieve a level of sophistication beyond many, if not most, onsite class discussions.

Message boards, by their very design, provide a complexity of audience: students are writing not just to the teacher but to each other. While negotiating the multiple audiences of a message board, students can practice invention skills, take risks, and develop their own authoritative voices. They aren't just writing to please you; most writing teachers are familiar with that sense of writing indifference that Britton and his coauthors discussed, in which students' apathy can manifest itself in a piece of "audience-less" writing (65). In addition, students are writing all the time on the message boards. I want my students to learn how to incorporate writing into various aspects of their thinking and learning, not just how to write dutiful college papers. Message boards can be a tremendous pedagogical tool to help them see the writing-learning link, and as Susan McLeod pointed out, they can learn from each other in a more active way (343). Also, with message boards, conversational digression can become an asset instead of a problem. Joseph Ugoretz commented on the value of digression in message board conversations:

> When teachers and students, like Frost's narrator in "The Road
> Not Taken," encounter two roads that diverge, asynchronous
> discussion allows them to avoid being "sorry that I could not
> travel both / and be one traveler." In asynchronous discussion,
> it is possible to diverge, to digress, and to acknowledge all the
> different kinds of "traveling" that are involved in learning.
> (par. 21)

That tantalizing digression that we might miss in an onsite class
can flourish on the message boards, assuming an importance
that you and the class can determine as it develops. (Recall John
Dewey's comment, "Perhaps the greatest of all pedagogical fail-
ures is the notion that a person learns only the particular thing he
is studying at the time" [49].) Message boards aren't perfect, of
course. Faigley discussed how these conversations might devolve
into chaos because they are so free (190), and when poorly man-
aged, students can certainly dodge engagement in the course. But
as long as you curb hostility or triviality and you provide clear
guidelines and a solid level of presence and engagement, you'll
find this a powerful environment when helping students learn in
your OWcourse.

Guideline 21: The asynchronous technology of message boards
can create a powerful and effective writing and learning environment for your students.

In my ten-week online classes, students write dozens of "official" posts, creating thousands and thousands of words in addition to the longer writing projects. These conversations have
been strong; in some cases, brilliant. As Collison and his coauthors
said, "inquiry in dialogue" for these participants "emerges from a
course design that enables them to *construct their own knowledge*,
together. The facilitated online discussion is the container for this
construction of meaning and useful outcomes" (3). Indeed, my
first-year students think hard about topics ranging from changes
in the science curriculum to explications of literary works. They

learn to make a forceful point in a succinct way. They learn to accept criticism gracefully, even when it comes under the glare of their peers' eyes. They practice careful reading, because arguments in an online setting often involve considerable rhetorical precision. They continually practice the difficult skill of using evidence—including direct quotes from other posts—to help reinforce their positions. By using message boards, I provide students with many low-stakes opportunities to write, helping them practice and refine their thinking through writing. And they use their writing to develop a point, building authority while speaking not just to me but to their peers. Perhaps most important, I think the kind of writing they do in these environments—short, mini-arguments to a diverse audience—better prepares them for the writing many of them will do as professionals (for support for this argument, see Jim Henry's *Writing Workplace Cultures*). The students often have a community learning experience that surpasses their onsite courses, knowing their "online co-learners more deeply than they would in a class where they would all be physically present with each other" (Hanna, Glowacki-Dudki, and Conceicao-Runlee 25). For example, at the conclusion of my winter 2009 persuasive writing OWcourse, one student said to her classmates, "Just wanted to say that you guys are awesome and this online English course enabled me to feel closer to my classmates, more so than a lecture. Thanks so much guys!"

Creating a Persona to Generate Conversation and Knowledge

In Chapter 1, I discussed creating your persona as an online writing teacher. That persona will help you as you interact with students electronically, and it will play a major role in the dynamic environment of the message board. In *Facilitating Online Learning*, Collison and his coauthors provided a useful framework for constructing a persona in this environment. They urged instructors to remember that the goal as a message board facilitator "is to clarify and extend the thinking of other people" (104–5), and they encouraged the adaptation of different voices to facilitate this role: "By consciously using *different* voices, you'll be reminded that the purpose of any composition as an online facilitator is to illuminate the thoughts of others, not to cleverly or entertainingly craft a position that puts you on center stage" (120). In Chapter 1, I introduced these voices, and I define them more clearly next, as they are useful in helping shape the way you interact with your OWcourse students on message boards. Say, for instance, that I set up a message board **thread** addressing issues of civic responsibility, specifically asking to what extent individuals are responsible to contribute to society. This example is based on conversations I had in my winter 2008 persuasive writing course using Nancy Wood's text, *Perspectives on Argument*. It was a particularly interesting conversation because many students believed strongly that individuals are solely responsible for their place in society, and I work from that premise here.

- ◆ **Generative guide.** The generative guide provides a spectrum of positions to indicate different avenues of questioning students might pursue in a conversation. As a generative guide, I start the conversation with a prompt that describes, based on our readings, the different positions regarding this issue: Who is responsible for the welfare of disadvantaged people? Government? Charity? The people themselves? How much should individuals be responsible for contributing to the greater good?

- ◆ **Conceptual facilitator.** A conceptual facilitator might resemble the voice of a lecturer but instead focus on elements of participants' postings and perhaps the course readings, not just on delivering content. In this capacity, after a few opening posts, I make sure the issues are clear in both the posts and our class readings. In a class this might resemble lecture, but in the message board environment, I build the content from not just the course but the student texts.

- ◆ **Reflective guide.** The reflective guide restates, with different emphasis, elements of a message or sequence of messages. The conversation begins with many people criticizing the plight of the poor and disenfranchised. "Why can't they find success in America?" many students ask. As a reflective guide, I try to change the us-versus-them theme arising on the boards, and I ask students to consider the different factors that might contribute to success. In fact, I ask, "What is success?"

- ◆ **Personal muse.** The personal muse might offer a personal internal dialogue about central issues. Building on the work I did as a reflective guide, I act as a personal muse by writing about the factors that led to my own success in life. I then invite students to think about factors that have contributed to their ability to attend college.

- ◆ **Mediator.** Mediators try to assess participants' unstated reasons for their reactions; in doing so, however, they do not avoid argument tension altogether. The civic responsibility example is particularly interesting in demonstrating the role of mediator. Students' positions might be informed by their unconscious feelings for the poor. Can I tease out the reasoning behind their positions to shed light on them?

- ◆ **Role play.** A role player can assume the voice of different characters, perhaps drawing on tales of personal experience delivered from a different role. The role player can successfully use the power of the Web in an asynchronous conversation. As a role player, I can provide examples of real-world people and how they have responded to the call for civic duty. I can even be someone I am not, taking a contrary position based on the stances I see being expressed on the board. (See Collison 106–17 for discussion of these terms.)

This collection of personas that Collison and his coauthors describe presents just one range of options for how you might envision yourself as a facilitator of online dialogue, and you can see how these voices overlap and complement each other. Having a sense of the different approaches you might take, and knowing when to use one over another, will help you maximize the conversations in your course.

Guideline 22: Remember that in the written environment of the message board, you will likely assume different voices and roles.

Joining the Conversation: You Need to Be Involved, but How Much?

Regardless of *how* you approach the message boards, you will want to figure out ways to push students' thinking; I believe that requires you to be involved. Janet Eldred recognized nearly two decades ago that productive exchanges in e-communications do "not emerge automatically" (56). Instructors might have different feelings about what is an appropriate level of involvement, but I believe that your responsibility as a teacher includes being a regular, engaged participant in students' online conversations. Collison and his coauthors offered three principles for effectively moderating message boards:

1. "Moderating takes place in both a professional and a social context" (5).

2. "The style of 'guide on the side' (vs. 'sage on the stage') is most appropriate for leading a virtual learning community" (7).

3. "Online moderation is a craft that has general principles and strategies—that can be learned" (12).

Following that, I'll offer a straightforward guideline:

Guideline 23: Although you don't need to be the center of conversation, you need to be involved with your students' asynchronous conversations.

One consequence of not being involved is that you risk allowing students to have the "Whoosh, It Went Right By" feeling (Collison 166). Students who see their posts disappear into a teacher-less void might shut down in the class. Sandy Hayes noted that teachers' participation in responding to posts serves various roles, including that teachers' comments model "peer review talk" for students and help the instructor build relationships with each student (72).

Although you should be involved, the level of that involvement differs, both among teachers and from conversation to conversation in a particular class. Don't go to the other extreme of hijacking the dialogue (Collison 166), as that might lead students to shut down in another way. One of the tough parts of conducting message board conversations is that you must participate in the conversation but resist the urge of being constantly drawn into discussions when they are irresistibly good—which, I warn you, happens often. In her oft-cited book about distance learning, *E-Moderating*, Gilly Salmon offered this *just right* principle for e-moderators: they should provide "enough, but not too much, intervention," which as a rough guideline should be not more than one in four messages from you (125).

Indeed, the problems with underparticipation are probably obvious, but there are reasons to guard against overparticipation as well. If you have one hundred or more students, you will burn out quickly if you read carefully, think about, and comment on every post. Luckily, in this environment, you don't *need* to comment on every post, because students do much of that work for you. I agree with Salmon that it is sounder pedagogically to avoid commenting on every post or even every conversational thread. Let the students roam. Let them sustain the conversation with questions and comments. In onsite classrooms, discussions can easily take the form of a teacher's question, a single student's response to the teacher, and then on to the next teacher question, a pattern "in which teachers ask test-like questions and students give short, test-like answers" (Cazden and Beck 165). Students rarely talk to each other. In the online environment, the same structure could develop if you are overzealous about responding, so choose your responses carefully.

The decision about when to comment must match the way you envision your role on the message board. Working from Collison's categories for constructing a persona earlier, I comment on message boards for these purposes:

- **To raise a question.** Acting as the generative guide, conceptual facilitator, or reflective guide, I often will respond to a batch of posts on a given thread with a question. Normally, as I go through the posts, I write questions that come to me in a separate notes area, usually in a Word file (so I can just copy and paste). Sometimes I hold off on a question for a day or two to see if the students arrive at it themselves.

- **To respond to a direct address to me.** I always respond when a student directly brings me up in the conversation. I want students to respond to their colleagues when they are directly addressed as well.

- **To state my position.** I *like* being part of the message board conversations. Not all teachers will. But on numerous occasions I have written long posts. I do my best to remember the rhetorical situation and not come off as a windbag—unlike in the classroom, students online are not captive to our "sage on the stage" delivery. If I am writing in self-serving ways all term, they simply might not read my posts. Instead, I try to offer direct commentary on the conversation and make useful general observations that apply to the lessons I hope to communicate during the term. Although I don't want to fill the boards with my propaganda, I don't shy away from adding my opinion to the conversation. After all, content aside, I am the teacher, and as a conceptual facilitator or mediator, I should offer a smart, complex post now and again.

- ◆ **To model.** Posts can be models for the students. After all, we teachers have our own writing expertise. This modeling is another great advantage of the message board environment: think about how seldom we model other forms of writing that we ask of our students.

- ◆ **To summarize a variety of posts or positions.** Toward the end of the week, I act as a reflective guide, summarizing a variety of student positions in one post and, I hope, advancing the conversation. While doing this, I am also demonstrating to students how to interweave evidence from their peers into a post. I use this type of post often during the lull that sometimes occurs between **primary** and **secondary post** deadlines (see below for my methods of using posts).

- ◆ **To offer a correction.** This can be tough. While I try to be fair, I also keep in mind that I am the teacher. Sometimes a student has a fact or quote wrong. I try to be gentle and constructive, but I will correct mistakes made on the boards. I try to establish, on the boards and in the class culture at large, that everyone makes mistakes and the boards are a public place, so no one should feel embarrassed by an error. I get the sense that these students respond within this feeling of collective good—and I have yet to find a class that will not challenge me when they think I am out of line or incorrect.

The level of participation you choose will relate to your own comfort level, but I think your role is to participate and challenge the students, much as you would in an onsite course. One study of teacher participation in online forums categorized instructor responses into three categories: (1) cheerleading, or posting reinforcement such as "Great job!" that added no new information; (2) adding new information; and (3) questioning or challenging. The study found that challenging was more valuable than cheerleading in helping "move the conversation forward" (Stansbury, par. 10). Encourage your students with positive reinforcement, but if their comments always just pass by you—a person who is trained to help them write and think critically—will they really be pushing their knowledge in the course?

Ultimately, you need to be active in your course discussions, perhaps in line with Sarah Haavind's suggestion that the quality of learning that takes place in an online course is highly dependent on the skills of the discussion moderator, who must guide the conversation in a "restrained but effective way" (par. 2). Peter Albion and Peggy Ertmer added that "once the discussion has begun, the instructor plays a key role in *managing* the discussion: keeping the conversation focused while also moving it forward" (screen 7; italics added).

In the Teaching Materials Appendix, I provide an extended abstract of an annotated message board conversation from one of my courses.

Lay Out the Rules

Decisions about choosing voices and personas can be more akin to an art, but successful message board conversations also depend on providing students with clear-cut guidelines. An *eCampus News* article about teaching with forums noted, "Simply providing online discussion forums is not enough to keep students engaged in virtual courses, according to educators who are well-versed in online instruction: For real learning to occur in an online setting, virtual-school educators must establish clear rubrics and enforce rules for participation" (Stansbury, par. 1). Smith remarked that in a Web environment, "you have to focus on interactions by being more purposeful about creating situations for interaction among the students"—directions must be clearer and more specific than in the onsite environment (65). Message boards, and any other assignment, are most effective when students understand what they are doing.

> **Guideline 24**: To get the most out of message boards, make sure your instructions and expectations are clear and detailed.

How can you make message boards work best? First, the conversations should cumulatively count for something worthwhile. The message board discussions in my online classes are worth 25 to 35 percent of the overall grade (I discuss grading more in Chapter 12). I had to make a conscious and initially difficult effort to release some of the course weight from the major projects and place it with the message board conversations. Now, I am more than confident about the wisdom of that decision. The writing that my students create on the boards is serious, smart, and complex; plus, they do much of it under tight deadlines with the pressure of a varied audience. They learn a lot, and they deserve credit equal to that level of learning. Second, you must define carefully what you want—without being so rigid that you kill the conversation before it starts. Following are instructions about using message boards that I provide to my class in the beginning of the term. Although these rules are for online classes, I use similar rules in my onsite and hybrid courses, as message boards play a large role in those as well.

Conversations that we have via message boards will make up a major part of the work in this course. In most cases, I will pose a question or issue to you, and then you will respond to me or to your colleagues. The responses will form a useful conversation about the issues we are tackling. Please read the material below carefully.

1. **Rules for "official" posts**—These posts should be:

   • ***Essays***. Responses should not be one simple paragraph, and I expect them to reflect some reasoned thought on your part, thought beyond what you might put into a normal email or chat response. Think of them as mini-essays that help you make a clear, focused point. Remember, you're trying to develop your writing; these posts are great practice.

   • ***Detailed***. Each of your "official" posts must be at least 125 words. (Note: I'm not as interested in the actual word count as I am in the depth of your ideas. Obviously a post like "Me too!!!" doesn't qualify as an "official" post.)

- *Semiformal.* Your posts should contain some degree of formality: spell-checked, organized, etc. However, they will also be part of a dialogue, so in that regard, they will differ from an essay you turn in for a class. It is inevitable that we will take some time to reach a mutual understanding of the appropriate level of formality.

- *Referenced.* While you won't always need citations in your posts, you should look for opportunities to build your argument by referencing our readings, other sources, or your colleagues' comments.

- *Courteous.* We don't always have to agree, but no one should resort to flaming.

2. **Grading**—I will grade your "official" posts in accordance with these rules. In total, you'll be responsible for 30 "official" message board posts. I will evaluate each one on a 10-point scale:

   - If you complete them adequately, you will receive 8s.

   - If you go above and beyond the basic requirements of the assignments, you will receive 9s.

   - Very good—completed with a great deal of effort and thought—posts will receive 10s.

A message board post will receive a 7 or below if it

   - is too short.

   - shows little thought.

   - is excessively sloppy in terms of grammar, spelling, and mechanics, especially to the point that it was difficult to understand.

   - engages in personal attacks or other breaches of common online etiquette.

   - is late (see Course Policies).

3. **Reading**—You are responsible for reading all of the posts in the class, although you can obviously focus your attention on the threads in which you are directly engaged.

4. **Shorter posts**—Feel free to post as many shorter, informal comments on the message board threads

> as you like; for instance, a couple of lines to
> clarify a point or to state your agreement with
> another author's point of view. But remember the
> rules for "official" posts.
>
> 5. **Staying current**—One of your responsibilities in
> taking an online version of English is that you
> will make it a *daily* habit to check the message
> boards and stay current on the conversations
> taking place there.
>
> 6. **Extra credit**—Those of you who are diligent and
> become active members of these conversations
> will find that you will receive a high grade for
> the message board component of the course. If
> you post more than 30 "official" posts, you will
> be eligible for extra credit in the course (some
> of you may naturally find that you have more to
> say on some of our topics this term, so I want
> to reward you if you put in extra work on some
> of the message boards).

The rules aren't complicated, but they are detailed. This detail might seem restrictive, but I have found that simple constraints like multiple paragraphs and a word count give students a clearer idea of the expectations (a word count works wonders for not only message board posts, but assignments such as peer reviews). We are, in a simplified way, providing students with a better sense of the genre in which they are writing. For example, if you ask them for references (with the occasional reminder), students will meet you more than halfway. Build in the rules you think appropriate—while remembering that these posts are conversational pieces of writing—and you'll find that the students exceed your expectations. Most important, they will *know* your expectations. In general, I think that teachers' expectations are too often a mystery to students.

Secondary and Primary Posts

You can assign message board posts in many ways, but one method has worked well for me: have students think about their posts as *primary* and *secondary*. Basically, in my grading scheme—as in the earlier instructions—primary posts are about twice as long and worth double the value of secondary posts.

Posts should be conversational, and secondary posts help apply conversational glue to the discussions. If all posts are extended essays in response to my prompts, the message board becomes more a series of disconnected essays responding to the instructor's question than a conversation.

In the beginning of a term, you might want to carefully monitor students' primary and secondary contributions, but I find that once we get into the flow of the term, students don't need to differentiate their primary and secondary posts. You can just tell. Some students will start off with a secondary post, reserving their longer primaries for later in the week. If you don't want that to happen, you could use a different nomenclature, perhaps calling the secondary posts response posts. More often than not, I find that many students post more than is required once they are engaged in a conversation on the message boards. I give a little extra credit for extra posts, and in a recent first-year course, the students posted an average of seven extra posts per student to the message boards.

Deadlines

I have experimented with different schedules for deadlines, but for me, the message is clear: in any **FYW** class, you must have students adhere to clear deadlines for their posts. Avoid a one-tiered deadline. You don't want all posts due on Friday, for instance. You might get a pile of poorly conceived posts just written to meet the deadline. Since a core goal is conversation, you might not get what you want with one fixed deadline.

In line with my use of two types of posts, I use a two-tiered deadline system. I ask students to submit a number of primary posts (as defined earlier) on a certain day, say Wednesday. Then I ask them to post a number of secondary (or response) posts by Friday. Using these two levels helps to build a conversation. Students have time between the posting deadlines to think about the initial posts and respond to their peers—as do I. Eventually the students don't seem to need the deadlines; they just have an ongoing, rolling conversation that spans the whole week and sometimes carries over to the following week. But in the beginning, the two-tiered deadline system can help generate that kind of conversation. Or, if you aren't getting the critical mass of conversation that you seek, you could try a three-tiered deadline system: student posts could be due on Tuesday, Thursday, and Saturday.

Length

As you can see from my sample instructions, a simple thing I stumbled across as a teacher is creating a length requirement for posts. This was a surprisingly effective way to help students understand the message board genre as well as the rhetorical situation: how long was the post supposed to be?

Grading Posts: Don't Be the Bottleneck in the System

A key philosophy underlying my use of **informal writing** is simple: students need to write in low-stakes environments to improve their writing. This is an entrenched idea in many compositional approaches ranging from Peter Elbow to Chris Anson to Toby Fulwiler. Despite this, many well-meaning teachers, in the heat of the semester-long battle, inadvertently short-circuit this process by becoming the bottleneck in the system. Starting with good intentions, they slow the process by trying to read every word their students write, and then they grind the process to a halt by trying to reply to every word. This might *seem* like the responsible thing to do, but the ultimate effect for most of these teachers is a reluctance to assign any more writing.

When some teachers hear that I ask for several dozen message board posts from each student, they shake their heads, envisioning an impossible amount of grading. But it's not onerous for me. I described my grading scheme in the example instructions earlier, and in more detail it looks like this:

- ◆ I grade primary and secondary posts quickly, using 10-point and 5-point scales. Especially if you stress multiple paragraphs for primaries, it's easy to tell them apart. (Some students write *all* longish posts during a given week—so any that count as secondary posts already go above and beyond my expectations.)

- The baseline grade is 8 for primaries and 4 for secondaries; it's important to establish this baseline number.

- If a post is decent, it gets 8 or 4 points.

- If a post is deeply thought out, much longer, and more engaged, it gets 9 or 4.5. Although I can fall victim to the automated test scoring prejudice that favors longer posts, I don't automatically up the score because a post is long. A long, sloppy post or a long, redundant post does not charm me by its length; but because these posts are informal and numerous, I am swayed a bit by people who simply had a lot to write.

- Excellent posts get 10 or 5 points, and excellence does not mean perfection for these informal grades: I give plenty of 10s and 5s.

- Late posts, extremely short posts, posts with many errors or vacuous ideas—these get 7 or 3.5 points or lower. I also grade down for people who don't add much to the conversation.

Your own grading conventions, or quirks, will emerge. For instance, I demand that primary posts be more than one paragraph; I want some movement among ideas, even in short posts. If I see one paragraph, it can be no better than an 8. You might have similar guidelines in terms of penalties for length, number of spelling errors, or being off topic; and rewards for use of sources, references to previous posts, or use of course concepts.

You can record the grades in a spreadsheet or directly into a CMS gradebook (every CMS has something like a gradebook). It may be quaint, but I still record grades by hand into an old hard-copy gradebook, much to the bemused amazement of some colleagues (I might avoid this by having two screens/monitors connected to my computer, but that's a technology option few of us have). It's a quick way to record grades as I read, and it takes me only a few minutes to transfer manually a whole week of grades to my CMS gradebooks. You can take advantage of the built-in post-grading functions that your CMS might offer, but my system of primary and secondary posts is not well served by those functions. (See Chapter 12 for more about grading.)

I feel strongly that I am not abandoning my responsibilities by grading so—well, efficiently. I use message boards because they create opportunities for low-stakes writing. I recognize that I cannot be the bottleneck, especially because the boards easily allow the other students to be an immediate and often responsive audience. In fact, feeling professionally obligated to watch every word that students write (and at some point it really does become more watching than reading if you try to grade everything your students write) seems ill-conceived. Mentors and coaches do not hawkishly watch every move their charges make. They allow them to practice, make mistakes, and thus develop. The message board environment represents an elegant combination of theory and practice, as it creates an ideal place to allow such exploratory or discovery writing to happen. Help guide conversations. Read because what they are writing is enjoyable. Clip out (easily done in the e-environment) pieces of posts to make specific points. But don't short-circuit this writing opportunity because you feel you don't have time to read every word. That is not your job. Your job is to help them develop as writers, and you don't have to micromanage their process to do so.

A final comment about grading posts: I have never—really, this has never happened—had a student ask me why an individual post received an 8 and not a 9. There are so many grades in the 1,000-point scale in my classes that 1/1,000 of a point is irrelevant. Occasionally, a student will ask why he or she *always* gets an 8, and that allows us to have a dialogue about the requirements for posts, which helps the student's writing: maybe the posts are too short, too error-filled, unoriginal, or even late. The grade becomes a handy communication mechanism to facilitate conversation about improving work. Isn't that what grades should be for?

Guideline 25: Let your students write on the message boards. Don't be the bottleneck in the system.

Generating Prompts: How Do You Get Them Started?

In a fully online course, students have two to three primary posts and two to four secondary posts due each week in addition to other course work. I always offer students flexibility about the threads in which they can participate in a given week. Normally, I set up between three and seven prompts based on the readings, their progress on drafts, or other course material from that week. Because they have more prompts than posts due, they can choose where to engage. I expect them to read all the posts, yet they can decide on which threads to concentrate their energies. Some weeks, I create one mandatory prompt to which everyone must contribute, such as a prompt that asks them to post a topic for a project and then comment on other students' topics or a prompt that addresses a key lesson we reviewed that week, for instance logic or process.

This is very important: don't get too clever with your prompts. It's tempting to make up complex prompts with multiple constraints. I find that the value of message board conversations goes up when you start simple. Often, I just use a one-sentence prompt. This is another reason that you should be an active participant in the conversation: I often map out a series of questions, but I reveal them gradually, much as I would in an onsite classroom, while the conversation develops and deepens. Here are some examples of message board prompts and questions to a few commonly used readings in the FYW course:

For E. B. White's "Once More to the Lake"
Initial prompt: Why does White experience "the chill of death" at the end of his essay?
Question later in the week: How do his observations of his son connect with his thoughts about the cycle of life?

For Toni Cade Bambara's "The Lesson"
Initial prompt: What kind of lesson is the story about?
Question later in the week: Why does the narrator resist Mrs. Moore so strongly?

For Martin Luther King's "Letter from Birmingham Jail"
Initial prompt: Who is King's audience, and what strategies does he use to persuade them of his approach?
Question later in the week: How does King convince his audience that some laws are not just?

For George Orwell's "Shooting an Elephant"
Initial prompt: Why does the narrator shoot the elephant?

Question later in the week: How does the narration in the story help support the argument about imperialism that Orwell is making?

For an excerpt from Annie Dillard's *Pilgrim at Tinker Creek*
Initial prompt: Provide some examples of the kind of description used by Dillard.
Question later in the week: What does Dillard's description seem to indicate about the natural order of things?

<small>TIP: SAVE YOUR PROMPTS</small>

In the beginning of the term, start saving all of your prompts. Your CMS might allow you to reproduce templates that could include these discussion starters so you can copy them into another term, but you might also want to save them to a single file to use later if you teach the course again or use a different CMS. You can refine the prompts, and this is one of the many ways of leveraging the technology when teaching writing in an online environment: you can save hundreds of thousands of keystrokes.

Student-Led Prompts

You can also use student-generated message board prompts, or ask your students to moderate conversations. Conrad and Donaldson provided examples of learner-led activities (110–19) in which students take the lead in generating conversations and activities in a class. Students can develop prompts and then guide their colleagues through that week's discussion. You can take it a step further, as Katrina Meyer did. She investigated having students serve as judges/evaluators of each other's posts in an online graduate course, rating posts based on their value to their class. She came to several conclusions, including that "investigating the role of some students in the collaborative learning process recognizes their importance in influencing the performance of other students," so "both instructors and highly regarded students" influence the way the class proceeds (16). This also creates an ongoing feedback loop in the course that she found valuable.

These are just a few examples, but students can certainly participate more in your message boards. This is another area of the OWcourse where you can productively give them the reins to help foster a student-centered environment.

How Do We Know They Are Reading the Posts?

I discussed this topic in Chapter 7, and it's a tricky question without perfect answers. Here I offer several additional strategies to encourage students to read and stay current with the message board posts.

ESTABLISH REWARDS AND PENALTIES FOR ORIGINALITY AND PARTICIPATION IN THE DIALOGUE

My rules include the stipulation that posts should contribute to the overall conversation. If I post an opening prompt that asks a question, and seven students simply respond to it in similar fashion, by student seven I am giving 8s, even on otherwise good posts. This is one way to check that students are *building* on the conversation.

USE MESSAGE BOARD POSTS AS SOURCES IN PROJECTS AND ESSAYS

I often ask students to use class posts as sources in their papers and projects. I like this strategy, as I think that asking for this type of evidence addresses numerous pedagogical goals. Students must read the posts more carefully to find material for their particular writing project. They also begin to construct or consider authority in the course, as students who are peer reviewing a colleague's paper may find (with pleasant surprise) themselves being quoted, perhaps juxtaposed with "other" experts from the course texts. And they think about ways of incorporating alternative forms of evidence into their writing. In addition, using posts in this way can discourage plagiarism.

Of course, if you want students to use posts as evidence, then you must set up threads that are relevant to the project or essay topics you assign, but that is normally not a problem. For instance, say students are working on persuasive essays about the topic of intelligent design, and you asked them to cite their classmates' posts. You can use thread prompts and responses that would elicit opinions—such as the simple thread starter, "What do you think of the concepts of intelligent design?"—so they have opportunities to find opinions from classmates that are worthy of citation.

USE MESSAGE BOARD POSTS AS PART OF OTHER ASSIGNMENTS

Another way to encourage students to read is to use some informal assignments over the course of the term that draw back on the message board materials. I often use the informal assignment "My Favorite Post" (see Chapter 9 for an example). This assignment asks students to think about other posts they have read in the course, choose a favorite, and compliment that poster. I use a thread like this both at the end of the term, for someone who has been an overall excellent poster, and early in the term, for a particularly great post. In addition to helping them read, the assignment allows students to "pay it back" to each other. One advantage of using an assignment like this mid-term is that it can encourage better assessment. As Meyer noted of such "evaluative" assignments, "using an on-going evaluation process—such as 'best posts' or some other mechanism—brings a form of useful feedback into earlier stages of the course" (16). Incidentally, I resist the urge to give them my own favorite, although usually one or two stand out for me. When asked, I use the lame strategy I learned as the father of three kids: "You're all special. . . ."

CMS Tracking Functions

It has taken me a while to get here, but you should know that your CMS most likely has functions that help you track students' participation in the course. This can feel Orwellian, and in fact, I seldom use these functions, but they might do some pedagogical good by helping you identify empirically low levels of participation so you can notify students. The data will be obvious for those students who have barely checked in on the boards.

Other Types of Conversations

The focus of this chapter has been asynchronous communications through message boards. I think the pedagogical opportunities for the OWcourse are richest in this environment, and most new teachers can quickly and easily become acclimated to CMS-driven message boards. But there are many other options, and I consider them briefly here.

Listserv

You can do many of the things described earlier with a **listserv**, an email list to which you and your students subscribe. Messages sent to the listserv email address go to everyone in the class. Students can manage conversations by emailing the list, and you can sort conversations by subject. In terms of organization, a listserv seems inadequate when compared to message boards, but all the listserv requires is that students have an email address. So in that regard, it's simpler than a message board, as there is no login, and the messages go directly into a student's inbox.

Chat

Chat is a well-established method of online communication and certainly has its use for OWcourses. For FYW courses, I think chat has some limitations, because the focus of the FYW course is often different from that of other courses: content is not king. Because I am building the course through student texts, I want more time with those texts, and I want students to spend more time creating them. Also, multiple-user conversations on chat can quickly fall into chaos. In comparing the advantages of boards to chats, Hayes said, "Chatrooms are fast-paced and ephemeral. The threads of the discussion are all tangled together, which is not as much a problem for the **IM**-savvy students to follow as it is for us. Bulletin boards save all the discussion so it can be continued days or even months later" (72).

Teachers have found good uses for chat and synchronous

conversations in online English courses. Kathleen Carico and Donna Logan observed that real-time chats provide an alternative space for engaging reading in making meaning through literature. Katherine Simpson described a synchronous environment where five to seven students and a peer tutor work in an "office" (424). Simpson noted the dearth of commentary about synchronous environments, remarking that in her class synchronous discussion participants "felt much more positive about the course, their classmates, and the peer tutors," and likening this to students who don't miss many **f2f** classes. "I encourage those who want their online courses to have the integrity that face-to-face classes have," she said, "to try a synchronous discussion component and involve peer tutors who can extend the personal connection that we as social beings need to ensure that learning takes place" (429). Like Simpson, I sometimes use chat to talk to individuals or small groups of students about their writing. Most CMS systems have chat functions, and many sites by educational support companies, such as book publishers, provide options for students to converse in this way. Ko and Rossen offered helpful tips for "establishing effective synchronous communication," including limiting the size of chat groups to four or five participants, and allowing time for students to socialize and ask off-task questions (213–17). You can find uses for synchronous technologies, but for the bulk of the communication in an OWcourse, asynchronous methods like message boards seem superior.

Voice

Companies like Horizon Wimba are ahead of the curve on voice technologies, which can even be used to replicate the classroom experience by bringing all students together via audio and sometimes video tools. A number of people teach online courses in this way, and it's common for students and teachers to be linked in a virtual classroom facilitated by AV conferencing technologies. I am not highly experienced with these technologies because my approach to the OWcourse is to use asynchronous text-based technologies.

MOO *Environments and Avatar*

As I wrote this book, I understood that online communications are rapidly changing. I have recently begun experimenting with Second Life, a more sophisticated virtual world than older environments like the **MOO** (Multi-User Domain–Object Oriented). Millions of people participate in immersive networked gaming experiences. Educators have been working with ways to use these technologies, including Second Life, to provide virtual classrooms where *avatars*—representations of the users—can assemble and learn. These technologies, though imperfect for some educational uses, offer yet another way of facilitating classroom community and conversation. I have a Second Life avatar (and I even have a virtual desk for it), but up until now it has led a lonely, mostly neglected existence. Perhaps at some point I will put it into action to see how I can teach with it.

Guideline 26: Some interesting synchronous technologies exist out there; you can experiment with them as you develop as an online writing teacher.

A final word about these more "advanced" conversational technologies: many of them might seem to render the message board rather humble, but let's not get too far ahead of ourselves. The message board is still a superb, flexible, easy-to-use technology for the online FYW experience because it allows students time to read, think, and write. Basic message board technology also provides an easy, one-stop way for instructors to manage these conversations. Levine asserted that message boards don't just reproduce f2f conversations, but instead "support higher-order constructivist learning and the development of a learning community. . . . The discussion board has the potential to provide the basis for creating a climate whereby the learning process is not limited by the traditions of face-to-face instruction" ("Online" 68). By using this simple technology, you can set up your class to do many of the things you want in your first OWcourse term.

Pre-term Questions

◆ *What type of communication will you use?* Learn the basics of its operation in your CMS. If, based on what you have read here, message boards will work for most of your communications, then learn how to set them up. Don't feel pressured to lay out every thread prompt before the term starts. You'll be inspired as you proceed.

◆ *Do you have a grading scheme for these conversations?* Think about the way you want to evaluate student conversations. Chapter 12 might help you consider how your message board grade fits into the overall grading scheme for the term.

◆ *What kind of deadlines do you want to have?* Base those deadlines around times when you will be able to most productively read and respond to student posts. For instance, if you are often busy on Saturdays, don't have the deadlines fall on a Saturday. By the time you check the posts, the conversation will be over.

◆ *Do you want to try some of the newer synchronous tools?* If so, you'll want to think through your pedagogical objective and make sure students can "meet" you in that cyberspace classroom.

CHAPTER NINE

Assignments: Online, Student Texts Drive Them

In this chapter I describe writing assignments and strate-gies that are particularly useful online.

The online environment enables you to use innovative assign-ments that have your students' writing as the central focus. When you start to see the different kinds of texts that your stu-dents can produce in this environment, only your creativity will limit how you have students write and think. As I mentioned in earlier chapters, this ability to use many informal assignments can create a risk-friendly environment in which students can develop their writing, which is a function both of what the students are doing and of the way we look at and evaluate their work. Because they write so much online, we can free ourselves from tendencies to focus on error in our students' writing, because each assign-ment itself is only a small piece of that monolithic grade we must administer. In her notable article "Talking to Strangers," Elaine Maimon wrote, "Too often talking about commas becomes a safe substitute for teaching and demonstrating how writers behave" (365). To me, this kind of teaching seems a natural result of the tension between students and teachers when assignments are so important—we end up trying to find reasons to state the flaws as a way of justifying grades rather than working with student texts. In the **OWcourse**, as your students produce a variety of fascinating texts, you may find you can help them explore and take productive risks to develop their writing.

This chapter directly connects with the previous chapter's discussion of message boards, because many of the assignments I discuss here, especially smaller ones, can be easily administered on message boards; so you'll note a bit of redundancy. Because basic problems of text distribution and creation are addressed easily online—particularly when you use message boards—OWcourse teachers can focus on doing some of those interesting things that they felt were too difficult to execute logistically in onsite courses.

> **Guideline 27**: Students can write a great deal more in an OW-course if you provide them with short, interesting informal or mini assignments, many of which can draw directly from their own texts.

Assignments Small

One of my favorite aspects of teaching writing online is that I can have students mine their own texts and their colleagues' texts in small, informal assignments; the underlying philosophy is that it's good to give many grades in your courses, and the online environment facilitates such grading practices. The peer review and evaluation of texts doesn't always have to take place in the relatively high-stakes environment of a major project or essay. Online, students are consistently reading and thinking about each other's words and ideas.

Many assignment ideas below are based on the assumption that students are having an ongoing written dialogue. As you read in Chapter 8, message boards are an excellent way and place to have those conversations. Because you have a lot of text to work with, you can create assignments that ask students to draw on their own writings. Those texts are (1) easily available to students; (2) easily available to you; and (3) easy to manipulate (cut and paste, copy, insert comments, and so on). The potential of what you can do with these texts is considerable.

Self-Reflective Writings

Many **FYW** course assignments ask students to reflect on their own writing. You can ask your students to do a great deal of self-reflective writing through various technology tools.

PORTFOLIO LETTER

A portfolio with an accompanying cover letter or report is a common end-of-term assignment, with the letter itself being a minor grade. Online, the contents of that portfolio can easily be gathered and can represent a variety of genres, some electronic. Students can be asked to review carefully a term of message board posts, choose posts that exemplify certain traits in their writing, and write a letter narrative about how they navigated the e-environment with these posts.

POST PROOFS

I use this assignment to provide a vehicle for students to write about their own message board posts in my classes. I ask them to review several of their own previous posts and proof them, writing an accompanying metacommentary:

```
Subj: Post proofs
Hi all,
Note that everyone must post a primary post here.
     Go back over your own message board posts. Pick
two longish ones (probably primary posts) and cut
and paste them into a separate document.
     Now, go through them carefully, seeking out writ-
ing errors. Correct those errors or comment on them
in ALL CAPS. At the bottom of the document, write a
sentence or two about what you think about the posts
after reading them again.
     Cut and paste the whole thing into a post here on
this thread (don't attach a separate file).
Let me know if you have questions,
Prof. Warnock
```

Elbow said that as writers, we need to be tolerant of our own mistakes (38). You can certainly ask students to find errors in their higher-stakes, formal projects, but I think that puts unusual pressure on them. For instance, I sometimes ask students in the f2f environment to read out loud as a means of proofing an essay they are about to hand in—a nerve-wracking experience. With message boards and similar **informal writing**, they can write thousands of low-stakes words, and that low-pressure environment may be more conducive to their developing a sharp eye for error, removing their fear of finding mistakes in projects that are worth a significant part of their final grade.

Reviews of Other Students' Writing

The OWcourse is a kind of ongoing peer review, with students exchanging texts and commenting on each other's ideas throughout the term. In addition to peer reviews of major projects, which I cover in Chapter 10, you can assign a variety of assignments that ask students to take account for each other's writing.

MY FAVORITE POST(S) OR POSTER(S)

I described this assignment in Chapter 8. I typically assign "My Favorite Post" at the mid-point of the term: students must identify one especially strong post by another student. One advantage of this assignment is that it asks students to take a critical look at each other's writing. It also asks them to read each other's writing carefully: they must spend some time reviewing posts. Here is a sample assignment:

```
SUBJ: My Favorite Post
Hi everyone,
Please look back through the archives of our message
boards, and either pick one stellar post by some-
one OR identify a few examples by one person who you
think did a fine job all term writing on the message
boards.
    Clearly identify the post(s) so the rest of us
can find them, and then write why you think these
posts were outstanding. Did anybody really knock
your socks off? Do you remember any one post standing
out?
Looking forward to some well-earned compliments,
Prof. Warnock
```

I use a variation of this assignment at the end of the term, this time asking students to choose a favorite *poster* and comment on that student's corpus of work from the term:

```
Subj: My Favorite Poster
Hi all,
Everyone must post at least one primary post to this
topic.
    As we did a few weeks ago, I want you to look
back through the archives of our message board
threads this term. However, this time, I want you to
identify someone whose posts stood out for you all
term. Identify examples by this person, and use ac-
tual quotes to demonstrate the talent of this writer
and to provide evidence for your choice.
Give out some kudos,
Prof. Warnock
```

Specific Writing Techniques

You can use an informal assignment, perhaps as a message board post, to ask students to analyze aspects of their own writing. For instance, if you are teaching a class about argumentative writing, you can ask students to return to and mine their own texts to evaluate how they have advanced various arguments with their posts on the message. What types of tactics have they used? One assignment I use frequently, and with a surprising amount of success, is to have students share their "tricks of the trade" in terms of how they research or execute other aspects of the writing/thinking process:

```
Subj: Share your secrets
Hi folks,
I always lament the fact that we rarely talk about
writing in college. If you have some trouble with
writing, it's like a dirty secret that you're not
supposed to talk about. I don't like that, and I
think it's damaging to students who are trying to
develop themselves as writers.
    Let's take research. Where do you start? How do
you do it? What techniques do you use? How do you
keep everything organized? How do you remember how
to incorporate quotes?
    For example, when I'm looking through a book or
article and making notes (whether electronically
or on paper), I always jot down the page numbers
in the left margin of the notebook or to the left
of my Word file. Then I write my notes—some quotes,
some paraphrases—until I get to the next page of my
source, and then I put that page number in the mar-
```

```
gin and just keep on going. That way I never lose
track of what page my notes are from, and I always
know exactly where a quote came from without having
to constantly rewrite the page numbers in my notes.
I find it helps me keep things organized.
     I also get plenty of great (well, I think they're
great) ideas when I'm taking notes. I use the code
MO right in the notes to indicate that this is MY
OWN idea. I don't know how that got started—it just
did.
Let us know some of your research tricks,
Prof. Warnock
```

I worried this might be an unpopular thread, but instead students pounced on it. In fact, one term I received so many excellent responses that I gave students an end-of-term "gift": a synopsis of these strategies, which were extremely interesting and diverse. Note that I also share my own tricks, and we become co-contributors in building general course knowledge about research. You can use informal writing assignments to share your own practices about all sorts of writing areas, such as reading, process work, proofing tips, and collaborative strategies.

Challenge the Persona

One way to have fun with informal assignments is by creating alternate personalities. For instance, I created a persona named Dr. Logoetho, who makes exaggerated claims, which students are invited to refute on the message boards. I try to bait them to see if they can remain logical and poised in the face of an unreasonable interlocutor:

```
Subj: Challenge Dr. Logoetho?
Dear students,
We will have an occasional visitor in our class, Dr.
Logoetho. Shockingly, Dr. Logoetho has never been
defeated in an argument. He has decided to test his
undefeated streak against you this week with this
argument (from his own hand, of course):
     "I think the whole debate about steroids is over-
blown. I guess kids shouldn't be encouraged to take
steroids, but I think that anyone else who wants to
should be allowed to take steroids. After all, life
is about finding advantages. Why should steroids be
```

```
any different? If you want to take steroids to bulk
up or run faster or if you are a professional ath-
lete, then I say go to it. It's nobody's business
if you want to take a substance that may harm your
health down the line—and I'm not even sure that's
even been proven."
     Well, if you want to take on Dr. Logoetho, go to
it—but make sure you use your evidence.
Good luck,
Prof. Warnock
```

These characters might argue without evidence, use logical fallacies, or debate from emotion. At the end of the week, we review—using specific student textual examples—the students' responses. Have they used evidence-based counterarguments? Have they maintained poise? Have they sought logical flaws in Dr. Logoetho's stance? Because the character is not me, the personal aspects of the argument are removed, and the texts students create become the centerpiece of often lively debates; as Dr. Logoetho, I do not easily go down in an argument.

Peer Review

Peer review is a significant enough component of the OWcourse that I spend all of Chapter 10 on it, but I mention it here because I grade peer reviews as components of students' informal writing grade. In my 1,000-point scale, peer reviews are double-strength, or 20-point, informal posts.

Using Learning Module–Based Assignments

The topic of learning modules is covered in depth in many books and websites about online learning, and it may fit here more neatly than in Chapter 4, which was about content. In Chapter 4, I pointed out that a CMS offers you opportunities to package a variety of different learning materials in one place. This allows you to bundle readings, video, quizzes, and other materials together and create an interesting small assignment. Here are a few examples:

Logical Fallacy Module

This module helps students understand logical fallacies, using these ingredients:

◆ A reading about logical fallacies from the textbook or handbook

◆ A reading I supply that contains a large number of logical fallacies (I often use some writing by Rush Limbaugh for this purpose)

The assignment output for this module:

◆ A message board post in which I ask students to identify fallacies from the reading I supplied, discuss why they are fallacies, and possibly address them

◆ A message board post in which they describe a fallacy from a popular commercial

Wikipedia Module

At Drexel we have been using a version of this module for several years, as it provides us with a great way to discuss the popular website and the value of the evidence students can find there. The ingredients:

◆ A YouTube video response to **Web 2.0**

◆ A cartoon from the Web about a supervillain rewriting a super-hero's Wikipedia entry (a Penny Arcade cartoon about Skeletor and He-Man, in case you're interested)

◆ An *Atlantic Monthly* article about the collective "hive" of Wikipedia-driven knowledge

◆ An *Inside Higher Ed* article about teachers taking a stand against Wikipedia

◆ A reading in the students' handbook about evaluating websites

The assignment output for this module:

◆ A primary message board post that asks students to analyze a Wikipedia page as a source by choosing a Wikipedia entry about which they have expertise, and critiquing it on the basis of its quality as defined by the handbook and its content

♦ A secondary post responding to a classmate's primary post

♦ A primary post asking students to review Wikipedia posting rules and to write up a *stub* (a kind of starter article) about a topic *not* covered on Wikipedia—this can be awfully challenging; they post to the message board, and they can actually post to Wikipedia if they like

♦ A secondary post responding to a classmate's proposed stub

Another advantage of creating learning modules is that you can leverage the technology to recreate them easily for other teachers (see Chapter 15).

Have Students Investigate Your Writing Process

Because you can easily post documents in any organizational form you like, you can do something many teachers would like to do in onsite courses: model your own writing process struggles. I once posted nearly a dozen drafts of a newspaper op-ed I wrote with a colleague. Each draft was accompanied by a brief note about where we were in the process. Students wrote on a lively message board, commenting on what they noticed about our collaborative process. You can also explore the possibilities of video, using a **screen capture** video to illustrate your own mistake-laden writing process so students can see how it works for you.

Assignments Big

If you've been whirlwinding your way through this book, wondering where you will find a comfort zone in your migration to online learning, feel better knowing that the main writing assignments in an online class can remain similar to those you have used in onsite teaching. There are nuanced ways to present major writing projects in the online class experience, but you don't need to reinvent the wheel: your well-designed projects can be migrated into the online classroom. Of course, some things you might want to think about or do differently, but initially, you don't need to change too much. Below are a few ideas for some of the larger assignments in your class.

Guideline 28: Major assignments can be altered in the OW-course environment, but you can often assign larger projects much as you have done in onsite teaching.

Journals and Notebooks Online

Journals are a mainstay in the FYW classroom, and you can maintain a journal in your OWcourse, but you can move it to an electronic format using one of the methods below.

◆ **Blogs.** I ask students to keep journals through weblogs they create on one of the many free **blog** applications on the Web. If you type *weblog* into a search engine, you'll see dozens of options for creating a free weblog. I provide the students with prompts each week, and they journal as they normally would, although the blog format has advantages: I never have to collect a back-breaking pile of journals, and the students can share the weblog address with classmates and friends. You can make the journal a private document, between you and students, or a semipublic document. My weblog assignment is in the Teaching Materials Appendix. I have been using blogs since 2002, and I have yet to encounter a student who could not set up one.

◆ **Email entries.** Simply ask students to email journal entries to you each week, using clear subject lines so you can have a folder for each student. This lets you have a one-on-one dialogue with students and avoids the paper chase.

◆ **Word document.** Students can keep journals in a Word document, and you can periodically ask them to post the documents to an assignment dropbox for your review.

◆ **Message board journal thread.** Many message board applications have a journal option that creates a thread viewable only by you and the student. This is another easy, paper-saving way to have a one-on-one dialogue with students.

Again, one advantage of these methods is that the journals, if you desire, are more easily sharable.

Process-Oriented Assignments

Because you can maintain your major assignments in much the same format online, I won't go into too much detail about them, but I will mention that the online environment especially might allow you to create major assignments that capture the process of students' writing. You can craft a variety of assignments that draw on students' work in the process of creating a finished project. One of my favorites is the *progressive cut assignment*, which might not initially win you many friends among your students, but which will help them understand the value of process and cutting. I use an assignment design similar to this:

◆ Assign a first draft with loose guidelines, such as "write an argument about a topic of your choosing." The key is length. Ask students to write an argument about any topic they like, as close as possible to 1,000 words.

◆ Next, have students complete a peer review, unveiling the directions only after the drafts are in. The key task in the peer review is to help the reviewee with the second phase of the assignment, which is to cut.

◆ In phase two, have students cut the word count from 1,000 to 500 words. (At this point I am still not involved with reviewing the drafts—remember, don't be the bottleneck.)

◆ After the 500-word version is submitted, ask students to reduce the project to a final one-page, 250-word op-ed piece.

As you might imagine, students are often up in arms after seeing their precious words bleed away, but I follow up this assignment with a message board conversation about the process—during which I give them the chance to voice their loathing for their instructor—and I am struck by how many of them understand and appreciate the value of the assignment. The grade largely depends on their ability to work through the process of cutting and meeting the deadlines and word counts.

Plagiarism

I don't wish to be a killjoy, but you must consider that the assignments in the OWcourse will be presented in whole on a class space, so someone could use the easy reproducibility of the digital environment against you. Fortunately, there are many ways to help avoid this, starting with intelligent assignment design (see Chapter 15).

Multimodal Opportunities with Assignments

In an informal review of FYW programs around the country conducted with research assistant Michelle Pagnani, we discovered that an increasing number are using **multimodal** assignments. The OWcourse might be conducive to using such assignments, because you are already presenting students with electronic means of submitting and presenting their work.

Guideline 29: When you develop major projects in the OWcourse, think about how students might include multimodal components in those assignments.

Students can work in different genres, such as producing a text-rich PowerPoint instead of a word-processing document. They can create virtual posters or websites that combine text and graphics. They can include video and audio as components of their work. At times, I think instructors feel that writing courses veer away from writing through the overuse of other media, but good assignments can blend different media, all fastened with the glue of writing.

Ong said that it is "bad pedagogy" not to teach the grapholect, which has greater resources than the dialect (108), and NCTE has honed a definition of twenty-first century literacy, describing multiple literacies often through technology: "Because technology has increased the intensity and complexity of literate environments, the twenty-first century demands that a literate person possess a wide range of abilities and competencies, many literacies. These literacies—from reading online newspapers to participating in virtual classrooms—are multiple, dynamic, and malleable" (par. 1). Much as you can deliver material to students in multiple ways, so too can their assignments reflect multimodality, as they can intertwine text, audio, video, and graphics into writing projects that better reflect the type of work they will be asked to do in a dynamic, media-rich culture. Although I touch on this topic only briefly here, you can use the vehicle of the OWcourse to help your students work toward this kind of proficiency and become learners who develop what Cynthia Selfe in 1999 called a *critical technological literacy* (144), understanding the role of technology in their literacy practices.

Dropboxes and Other Ways of Receiving Deliverables

You'll need to consider how you want to receive assignments in your online course. This may be a significant change for some teachers who are accustomed to receiving materials as hard copies. Every CMS has built-in assignment dropboxes. Frankly, some are clunky. You could simply have students email files to you, although those files can rapidly eat up space in your email folder (if space is an issue), and you might open yourself up to computer viruses and worms. Message boards include ways of attaching files, so you could also use that method to collect your students' files. I think the ideal is a one-click download that puts all of the files into one folder on your hard drive. Interestingly, Turnitin offers such functionality, and it serves as a great dropbox.

Format

Make sure you are clear about the format in which you want to receive files. Students find all kinds of odd formats to submit their work. Specify that you want one of several different formats, and make sure that students adhere to those formats.

Pre-term Questions

◆ *What are the main projects in your course, and how will informal work accompany those projects?* This may be a significant shift in the way you think about your teaching, so consider how you can integrate various process assignments into your grading.

◆ *How can you rethink your traditional grading scheme?* A large percentage of the course grade can be generated from students' informal work. This allows you to capitalize on the multiple texts that can potentially be created in an online class.

◆ *What kind of informal assignments might you use?* You can go from one extreme, grading everything individually, to the other extreme, asking only for an end-of-term portfolio; but you can still weigh the value of having many assignments in your OW-course syllabus. Tap into some resources. MERLOT (Multimedia Educational Resources for Learning and Online Teaching), for instance, has a variety of learning objects you might use in your class.

◆ *How do you want to receive assignments?* Plan ways to receive and return assignments, and decide how you will provide feedback.

CHAPTER TEN

Peer Review: Help Students Help Each Other

This chapter focuses on peer review, especially on the use of technology tools in the electronic writing classroom to help clarify the aims and potential of peer review.

In *Virtual Peer Review*, Lee-Ann Kastman Breuch defined *peer review* generally as students "responding to one another's writing for the purpose of improving writing"; she then defined *virtual peer review* as "the activity of using computer technology to exchange and respond to one another's writing for the purpose of improving writing" (10). With virtual peer review, she wrote, the online interaction "reverses the primacy of oral over written communication so that written communication is king" (2).

Peer review as a teaching strategy is so entrenched in composition that it might almost serve as an emblematic practice of composition, and as with other practices in the **OWcourse,** the transition to a completely written peer review environment makes this common practice perhaps even more important online than in onsite instruction. Yet in perusing books about online instruction, I found that peer review is often glossed over or treated in a page or two, and the emphasis is often on evaluations among members of teams. I had difficulty deciding where to place a conversation about peer review in this book, because it overlaps with so many different areas. But like Sandra Sellers Hanson and Leonard Vogt, who said specifically of peer editing, "It is appropriate for students in a writing class to be involved in the process of peer editing since editing is so important a part of good writing" (577), I decided that peer review is important enough to writing class pedagogy that in a book about online writing instruction, it warrants its own chapter. One reason for this is that despite how ubiquitous peer review is in the **FYW** class, even some experienced teachers have trouble making it work consistently.

However, even if your peer review practices work well, you might find that technology becomes an effective partner in helping you conduct peer reviews in new and potentially more effective ways; the many benefits have been recognized by others who contemplate peer review in the e-environment. One obvious benefit is that the author of the project being reviewed gets feedback; but as Ko and Rossen noted, peer review helps the reviewers themselves to "view the criteria for an assignment with fresh eyes" (122). You can even ask reviewers to use rubrics or other evaluation guidelines that are close to the way you will evaluate the project. As another advantage, Breuch observed, "virtual peer review encourages writers to take deliberate control of technologies and to think strategically, not just as writers, but as technology users" (5). When coupled with communication technologies such as message boards, peer evaluation online is ongoing, and student writers must think not just about the message but about the medium of interaction. Perhaps most important, the tool you use to conduct the review can guide you and your students as you rethink the process.

Guideline 30: Peer review is a standard FYW practice that can operate in an enhanced way using the technologies of the OWcourse.

In discussing *intensive peer review*, Martin Nystrand said that students who are taught by peer review "make more progress in writing" for a variety of reasons, including that they see revision more as "reconceptualization" than as editing; view readers more as collaborators than as judges; and see rewriting more as "improvisation and experimentation with ideas and text" (1). As I frequently tell my students, their peer review work is often some of the most "real" writing they will do in the course. They are writing with a concrete purpose: to help their colleagues produce a better written project. When they take this task seriously, they are often engaged in the most "transactional" (Britton 85) writing they will do all term, providing ideas that their audience may immediately use.

Email Reviews

Keep in mind that if you have solid review guidelines, online peer review can be as easy as providing some guidance and then asking two students to exchange documents and reviews via email. Although some technology observers predict the death of email (in his **blog**, Dave Pollard called email one of "12 Tools That Will Soon Go the Way of Fax and CDs"), as of now it still remains a frequently used communication technology. You would just need to provide students with access to each other's emails, whether the email is embedded within your **CMS** or in students' standard accounts. Follow the process by having them carbon copy you on their email interactions. To pair up students, post or email a list of partners, organizing them alphabetically. They can exchange the draft documents by attachments via email, but I think it's better for them to retrieve the documents from a centralized place, such as the course CMS.

Message Board–Facilitated Peer Review

Setting up message board peer review can be simple.

- ◆ All students post their project drafts to a message board **thread** that you have set up for this purpose. Now everyone in the class can easily access each project.

- ◆ After the projects are posted, you can post a list of reviewers, generating that list in any way you like (it's important that students aren't late with their drafts).

- ◆ Next, list a series of criteria on the message boards, or use some other format. I helped develop Waypoint, Web-based software with a robust peer review function that allows reviewers to use the same rubric their teacher is using.

◆ Reviews can be sent to the reviewee via email or some other private channel; or made public, which works especially well if you're asking students to review more than one project and if you want the reviews to build into a *conversation*, perhaps even with the author's responses.

Message board–facilitated peer review has many advantages, some simple and obvious, others more nuanced.

Distribution of Documents

Distributing documents is a baseline problem to solve in conducting a good peer review, especially in the OWcourse. One or two absent students can complicate your efforts as you scramble to reassign papers based on those students. Even onsite, you must rely on students to bring sometimes multiple copies of their drafts to class—accurately collated and stapled! The shuffling of papers can take up too much time at the beginning of an onsite peer review class session.

You can easily use message boards to simplify this process. Because almost all message board technologies allow users to attach documents, you have a way to let everyone in the course post their documents so that everyone else, including you, can access them. Then, you can use the boards to post a distribution scheme and peer review instructions. I think peer reviews work well in this format, and others agree. As Hayes said bluntly of her own teaching, "Using the bulletin board has increased the efficiency and quality of peer review" (71).

Peer Review Groups

Most CMS packages have a group or team function that allows you to assemble students into groups (see Chapter 14). You can use these groups to replicate the group environment of a peer review circle. Students can post their drafts here, and the entire group can check in with reviews, based on criteria that you create. You can even keep the same students together working as a peer review group throughout the term. These peer review groups require everyone involved to write and read carefully—precisely what we're seeking in a writing class. You could match them up with different partners within the group or use the peer review method of one student on the "hot seat," posting his or her project while the others take turns critiquing. Keep in mind that most CMS group functions allow for groups that are private for the members, so this can be a semiprivate space within the larger class, accessible to only you and the group members.

Using message boards, you can make posting a draft optional but a peer review mandatory. Thus, you'll probably have more reviews than drafts. In this format, I require subsequent reviewers not only to critique the draft, but to account for previous reviews in doing so, building a chain of either consensus or productively contradictory messages.

Blogs or Wikis

You can create a **wiki** or blog that begins with a student's draft, and the comments that follow are reviews of that draft. In a wiki, students can edit each other's posts, creating an interesting writing dynamic. You'll be building an interesting e-conversation about the draft, and each of the posts could also include responses, clarifications, and explanations by the author. The peer review dialogue can be organized chronologically or by subject.

Note that as with all OWcourse peer reviews, the use of a blog or wiki isn't so much about technology as it is about a conceptual approach to how you will conduct your reviews. The technology can guide you to an approach that you consider effective for peer review—wikis, blogs, or any other tools are simply the *interface* to put that approach into action.

Peer Review Software

Many software packages and programs can help you to conduct peer reviews. I describe two of them below. Note that many publisher sites have peer review capabilities; see in particular Bedford/ St. Martin's CompClass and Pearson's MyCompLab.

Waypoint

Waypoint (Figure 10.1) is a software product that I helped design, and I am a co-founder of Subjective Metrics, Inc., the company created to develop the tool. Waypoint is Web-based rubric creation software that allows you to conduct peer reviews using a rubric close to the actual guidelines you use to grade student work. Waypoint provides a way for students to respond in specific categories to peer review questions that you design, and it allows you to easily manage the process. You can create prompts that encourage complex student comments.

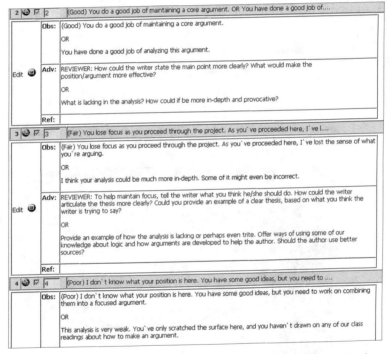

FIGURE **10.1.** *Example of a Waypoint peer review. The reviewer will select one of several options for the criterion of main idea/thesis for a position argument.*

Calibrated Peer Review

Calibrated Peer Review (Figure 10.2) is another Web-based program. It's designed to enable "frequent writing assignments even in large classes with limited instructional resources," and to possibly reduce "the time an instructor now spends reading and assessing student writing." The software facilitates a recursive process in which students develop competency in a set of review criteria, and after they "become competent reviewers," they evaluate their peers' writing in a double-blind process before returning to final revising on their own project (Russell 67).

Synchronous Technologies

Using a **whiteboard** with accompanying audio or chat (almost any CMS has these functions), you could conduct peer review

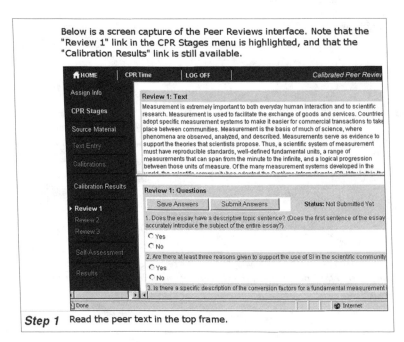

FIGURE 10.2. *Part of the Calibrated Peer Review process.*

like an onsite workshop in which you and the class look carefully at several student drafts. Explore ways of using the whiteboard space, chat, or voice technology to replicate that experience. Many free programs or tools on the Web, including Google Docs, and many publisher sites that accompany textbooks have the same dynamic, although I suggest that you first explore the options within your CMS.

Publisher Sites

It's worth noting that many composition textbook publishers have developed fairly sturdy sites that include tools to help facilitate sharing and commenting on student documents. Publishers are happy to work with you to demonstrate these tools.

Criteria and Guidelines

In the **WAC** workshops I have facilitated, I've often encountered someone who likens peer review to "the blind leading the blind." I think a teacher's success with peer review is directly proportional to the clarity and seriousness of the peer review instructions. Bruffee said that peer review is only useless if we believe in a Cartesian educational model, in which we impress knowledge on individuals. If instead we see knowledge as being created by a community of knowledgeable peers and that learning is social, then peer review makes good sense (646). We can use the OWcourse environment to reinforce the underlying message of peer review: writing is *not* an isolated activity. In this way, we can refute the flawed modernist metaphor of the lone writer in the garret, where "the garret hides the technology of writing" (Brodkey 397). Technological tools can help us foreground the social aspects of the writing process.

Peer review instructions must be clear. As with many other aspects of teaching, this fact might be even more important in the OWcourse. Make your peer reviews more effective by following a few guidelines:

◆ **Provide crystal-clear instructions.** Don't give students a pass to respond only with a binary good/bad choice about the writing they are critiquing. I sometimes talk to teachers who have had little success with peer review, and then I discover that they are asking students a series of binary response questions: yes or no. Similarly, if you give students only the general direction "Describe what you think about the essay," or an equally ambiguous instruction, the reviews might fall flat. Although you might build as part of your strategy a Peter Elbow–like knee-jerk response to a draft, you also need to provide clear instructions about how to elaborate.

◆ **Create a length requirement.** By doing this, I have changed my peer reviews. They are chunkier and more substantive, simply because I have asked students to write a certain number of words. This gives students a baseline rhetorical understanding of what this review genre should look like.

◆ **Don't allow an "answer the question" approach.** Even if the answers are not binary, you still should avoid reviews that allow students to simply answer the questions on a list. The peer review itself should be a solid, cohesive piece of writing that is graded on the informal scale in the course and that *incorporates* the language of the questions.

◆ **Make it clear that you want a critic, not a cheerleader.** Students can default to the comment, "This paper is great! All you need to do is _____," with the blank filled by something superficial, such as correct spelling or punctuation. Make it clear that you are aiming for more than that.

◆ **Create a clear response genre.** I like it when students write memos to each other. The memo is a simple genre that is useful for transmitting documents, and it works effectively for students to communicate their peer reviews. Make sure you give a clearly articulated means of communicating their ideas to the reviewer.

◆ **Grade the reviews.** As I discuss in Chapter 12, giving students lots of grades is one way of motivating them in the course while allowing them to take risks. If you grade peer reviews with an informal grade, you reinforce their importance in the class. As the teacher, I don't mind inserting myself into the dialogue and helping to reinforce some of the better points, while steering students away from the vacuous "Great job!" comment or one that is simply off track.

◆ **Don't be afraid to criticize the reviews.** If a review is off the mark, especially if it appears that the student didn't put any time into it, then say so to the reviewee. You can do this without being mean spirited.

Give Them Your Rubric

One thing you can do, regardless of how you conduct your peer reviews, is provide a way for students to see writing the way *you* will see it. This is one of the many advantages of using rubrics. By giving students a version of your rubric, you are establishing the requirements of the project. You might find it fascinating when they demonstrate the vocabulary built into your rubrics while they are discussing writing.

A Sample Peer Review

Following is a sample review from one of my classes. I try to make the instructions as explicit as possible. This was a message board–facilitated review, so in addition to these instructions, I provided a simple list matching reviewers and reviewees.

> Hi everyone,
> Please CAREFULLY follow the directions below to peer review a colleague's project.
>   At the bottom of this message is a list matching reviewers with projects. You will find the person's project posted in this topic (some people have posted twice, so make sure you look at the most current post).
>
> 1. When you open the project file you are to review, IMMEDIATELY re-save it by adding "review" on the end of the file name. (So if it's ScottWdraftproject1NFL.doc, you'll re-save it as ScottWdraftproject1NFLreview.doc).
>
> 2. Note below that you can make comments in the text, but do not delete any text.
>
> 3. After your review, you will EMAIL the newly saved file to the author and cc me (sjwarnock@ drexel.edu).
>
> Please write a 200-word review of the project, using the criteria below as a guideline. The review will take the form of a memo that you will write in the beginning of the project file, right above the head-

ing. Don't forget to include your name. Please don't just answer the questions below. Instead, use them as guidelines to help you write a 200-word memo.

- Does the project fulfill the assignment? Why or why not? (Hint: Get the assignment directions out to answer this question.)
- What's the writer's purpose?
- Does the writer account for audience effectively?
- What's the project's main idea/argument? Is this clearly worded?
- Are there counterarguments the writer has not addressed?
- Are there particular places where the writer would be well served to use sources?
- Are the paragraphs logical? Do they relate to the main idea?
- Comment on the grammar and mechanics. Do recurring, glaring errors interfere with the project's message?
- Name two main strengths.
- If this were your project, name two ways you would improve it.

Remember, the review must be finished by Wednesday night at 11 p.m. (see this week's **Weekly Plan**). Let me know if you have any questions,
Prof. Warnock

A Word about Text-Based Peer Review

When creating a peer review for your online class, remember that writing is hard work. Teachers struggle at times to communicate their precise feelings about a paper or project, so think about the pressure on the students. They have the challenge of carefully reading another student's project and then writing about it in a way that helps that colleague—and all directed to a student they may not have met. This is no small task. In fact, Conrad and Donaldson stated that the skill of reviewing "needs to be practiced more in an online environment than in a classroom-based environment because visual and aural cues are missing, so text-based criticisms, even when they are constructive, can be construed as overly harsh" (60). The idea is that students might need more guidance and practice in their online peer review skills.

You can use this inherent difficulty as a positive if you structure your peer reviews carefully, along the lines of the criteria above. Help students understand that they must carefully and tactfully advise each other, and explain to them that you understand the fundamental complexity of this writing task.

And One Final, Nettlesome Little Thing

Using electronic means of document dissemination means you have a lot of perfect replicas of student writing floating around the Web. Plagiarism is an issue. Breuch said of virtual peer review that it "may require finer distinctions with regard to collaboration, because the textual nature of the activity may raise issues of ownership and authority" (80). This is another reason that I prefer a closed CMS environment to an open one. Of course, the best defense against plagiarism is the assignment that embeds the student's work in the culture of the course, but as I discuss in Chapter 15, plagiarism checkers such as Turnitin are useful in thwarting that most obnoxious of cheats, the one who steals a whole paper. I think very, very few of my students would do such a thing, but I don't want to spend valuable time tracking down cheaters when I could be helping students improve their writing.

Breuch pointed out that electronic reviews of text are becoming increasingly prevalent in students' lives and in the world of work (12), and she added that using peer review in the e-environment "exemplifies . . . the tension we may feel regarding . . . moving to virtual environments" (56). It appears that students will continue to review and collaborate online, with their written words serving as the core means of communication. We can help them develop those skills through the OWcourse. The online version of peer review holds promise, because even if students are intimidated in a face-to-face classroom, "responding to an idea on a screen may relieve some of their anxiety and tension" (Stedman 25). As part of their regular practice, students should be commenting on each other's words and ideas. If we do a good job of structuring and encouraging these responses, we will have created a useful writing exchange environment for our students.

Pre-term Questions

♦ *How will you facilitate peer review in your class?* This is best done by thinking about what you want to accomplish. Should the reviews take place via message board? Via email? Via **synchronous** chat?

♦ *Do your writing project deadlines include room for review?* This might seem obvious, but make sure that your deadlines include time for a peer review cycle.

♦ *Have you included peer review in your grading scheme?* You should grade peer reviews, so decide how to include them in your overall grading scheme.

♦ *What criteria will you use for the reviews?* As discussed in this chapter, there are many tools at your fingertips. Spend time thinking about the criteria you will use for the reviews.

CHAPTER ELEVEN

Response: Give Lots of Feedback without Burning Out

This chapter will explore methods and strategies for one of the key parts of the writing teacher's interaction with students: response to student writing.

When you teach writing online, your methods of responding to students are forced to change, often for the better. In many cases, the change is mild: you begin typing in-text comments on a word processor instead of writing them hurriedly—and sometimes illegibly—in the margins. Similarly, you type a brief (but possibly longer than handwritten) end comment. Of course, the possibilities for innovation far exceed this. Digital response technology starts by helping us save keystrokes and time, but as with most of our teaching, it invites a rethinking of conventional response practices, essentially helping us reassess the crucial dialogue we have with students about their writing. For a more in-depth discussion of the dialogue between teachers and individual students, read Hewett and Ehmann's *Preparing Educators for Online Writing Instruction.*

> **Guideline 31:** Technologies of response can help you rethink the way you provide feedback to your students about their writing.

You can start with simple tools like **macros** (defined later) or pre-generated rubrics. From there, the technologies include tablet computers, Web-based rubric generators, commenting software, even voice recognition software or audiovisual comments—you'll find many tools to change the way you respond to student writing in your class. Because response is such a large component of what you do as a writing teacher, it's best to think about response strategies *before* you get that first round of drafts.

Note that I differentiate between *response* to student writing—a major part of our job in writing classes, and even more so in the online environment—and *grading*, which includes evaluating writing, giving quizzes, and calculating final grades. I discuss grading in Chapter 12.

TIP: Many of us are accustomed to double-spaced prose, but when you receive documents online, you can ask students to single space them. This means less scrolling as you read (about half as much, in fact). And you can change any student document into the format you prefer—another advantage of receiving documents electronically.

Let Them Know Who You Are: Talk Back (a Lot)

The first step in thinking about response in the **OWcourse** is to realize that your students will write a lot, and that you will be responding to them textually more than you probably ever have before. To create a rich textual environment of dialogue with your students, start by immersing yourself textually into the class. Hewett and Ehmann offered the same advice in online tutoring situations, suggesting that instructors take "account of the affective dimensions of the experience . . . [to] develop a rapport with the writer and [begin] the interaction with a friendly tone" (78). Especially at the start of the term, I am an active respondent to my students' messages. For example, in my email folders for my online classes, I include a *To* field for the emails contained there. I can't sort all messages by *From*, because almost all of the messages have the same sender: me. What do I mean by this? I nearly always try to have the "last word" in my email conversations with students, especially early in the term. I respond to them so that they'll know I've heard their question or comment; I am there to help them. "Good deal," "Gotcha," "Thanks for the message"—even a short response helps create the communicative fabric I consider integral to developing the relationship needed to help teach writers (especially first-year writers) how to improve their writing in the OWcourse. Doesn't this contradict what I've said about not being a bottleneck in the writing process? No—I'm talking here about conversational responses to *specific* student messages, not assessments or evaluations or interposing myself in student-to-student dialogue. I don't reply to everything, but I always reply to four kinds of messages:

- Emails to me
- Posts on a message board **thread**, like "Questions about assignments"
- Posts on a message board where students introduce themselves
- Message board posts or any other e-communication that directly addresses me

In the beginning of the term especially, teachers should respond a lot. Michael Smith and Jeffrey Wilhelm wrote that the implicit "contract" between students and their teachers includes that teachers should know students personally and care about them as individuals (99). In an online class, brief conversational links with students go a long way toward making them feel welcome and connected. When you teach writing, these feelings can build the mutual respect necessary to work with students on their core writing and thinking skills.

Think about what your active response achieves: you are fleshing yourself out as an *audience* for your students, an important pedagogical tool. We might take it for granted, but as students look us over in our onsite classes, they are often subtly—and perhaps subconsciously—gauging what we will be like when we read their essays (see Malcolm Gladwell's *Blink* for a fascinating conversation about our intuitive judgments and reactions). Online, students can feel detached, unless we capitalize on the textual-conversational environment of the online class and give them perhaps an even sharper view of who we are than they can get onsite.

So in week one, if you give students a message board icebreaker to introduce themselves (see Chapter 1), write back a lot. These bits of information place a sharper focus on you as an audience. After a series of responses, you will have given students a snapshot of yourself, and they will be better prepared for the writing ahead.

> **Guideline 32:** Respond a lot, especially early in the term. Let your students know you are there, and help them establish who you are as an audience.

Starting Simple

If you have never done any electronic commenting, you'll have a slightly bumpy transition, if for no other reason than you might find it hard to read all of the work electronically (an issue Christina Haas called the "text sense problem" [58]). Consider the long-standing image of the writing teacher: sitting in a café with papers stacked neatly on a table, quietly reading, and then writing comments by hand. That changes in the online environment—although you can still print out your papers if you choose to do so. You will often get your papers electronically, and you will return them electronically, so you'll need to find ways to comment electronically.

Some of what I discuss here about conversation repeats information from Chapter 8, as responding to conversation is a fundamental part of the OWcourse. The learning that takes place in these assignments and interactions is crucial to students' success in the class. A key philosophy in OWcourse response is worth stating again in a slightly different way:

> **Guideline 33:** Don't be the bottleneck in the system. In responding to students throughout the term, it's essential to remember this guideline. You want your students to write a great deal in the class. If at any point you feel overwhelmed and unable to respond to their shorter, informal assignments, then you need to adjust your expectations of how much you are going to respond.

You can allow students to write in many ways online. If they are all waiting for you to respond, you are slowing down the process.

You need to have some part in student conversations, and in many cases students can productively lead those discussions, but like any teaching strategy, you can take this too far. You are their teacher for a reason, and it's your responsibility to facilitate conversation in a way that helps build their writing and their thinking. Good teachers can facilitate discussions onsite or online that feature students prominently, but at times, students need your guiding hand. That might be even truer in the OWcourse, where your constructive comments can be not only about the subject of the conversation, but about students' actual writing. Through your responses, you want to achieve an environment in which all students have written a lot and are willing to have not just their ideas critiqued but the way they have delivered those ideas. This may leave you open to criticism: try giving students extra credit if they catch you making errors ranging from typos to unsubstantiated claims. If you're thick-skinned, this can be fun.

Keystroke-Saving Techniques

Although people have decried repetitive, mindless response commentary for decades (Nancy Sommers anticipated such objections in 1982 with her discussion of "rubber-stamped" commenting [152]), and sometimes rightly so, there is no denying it: we often say the same thing to many students on a given assignment. When you handwrote comments, your options were limited to reduce the amount of repetitive writing you did. You might have used a shorthand system (unfortunately, many of these now seem Byzantine) that linked students to a rubric or to an accompanying handbook. But when you type comments via computer, you can start immediately saving keystrokes in a constructive way.

A simple method of doing this is to use the macros available in word processor programs. Macros are shorthand commands that reproduce computer keystrokes. Describing how to set up macros is beyond the scope of my discussion here, but your word processor's help area can quickly guide you. Macros save keystrokes when you are making common comments. You can use an even simpler form of this process by keeping common comments in a file that you have open when you evaluate student writing; then you can cut and paste comments from the file to the student document. With macros, you can easily alter the comments to provide more focused response for a particular essay.

Macros do have downsides. For one thing, you could rapidly build up so many comments that you would have an enormous list to monitor. Perhaps you'd find an easy way to organize such a list, but it seems onerous to me. Also, recall that when using any kind of commenting strategy that reproduces keystrokes, you could slip into a boring, mechanical routine; students most likely would sniff out the inauthentic nature of your comments, which might disrupt your ability to help them improve their writing. The whole process could begin to feel like an assembly line. But it's important to note that falling into a routine is not an inherent characteristic of using such technologies; instead, it's the way you employ them. You can use common commenting macros to fill in the lower-level writing concerns (common sentence-level errors such as fragments, for instance) so you can spend more response time on higher-level issues. This seems like a reasonable trade-off, and I think it will resonate with teachers who have a hundred or more students.

Remember, you will read thousands upon thousands of student words. Anything you can do to responsibly limit your keystrokes is fine, as it helps stave off repetitive stress injuries, which are no fun when your life revolves around typing, as many of our lives do.

Rubric Software

The many different examples of online rubric creation software include RubiStar, RubricOne, Rubrics.com, and Waypoint. These programs allow you to create electronic rubrics, and the old paper rubric that gets used in early grades can be enhanced considerably with **Web 2.0** tools. You can develop personalized rubrics that capture exactly what you want to say, and in Waypoint, you can customize any comment as you create it, so you're not bound by pre-generated text. Rubrics have a variety of other advantages, including that you can share them with students so they can see how their work will be evaluated. And rubrics can serve as a framework for peer reviews, thus revealing your evaluation criteria to the students.

Alternatives for In-Text Comments

Regardless of how we evaluate student writing, most teachers use some form of in-text commenting so students can contextualize our advice. F2f, we write in the margins and in between the lines. As Lil Brannon and C. H. Knoblauch cautioned years ago, we must be careful not to colonize or commandeer a student's ideas (158), but we can work on different ways of writing comments to create the constructive response environment that can help them write better. Several approaches and technologies can help you with in-text response.

The most basic idea behind a comment is that students can see it. That was easy when you handwrote on a typed project, and perhaps a little trickier on a written exam or in-class writing (hence the teacher's use of the widely maligned red pen; sure, it's red, but the contrast makes it easy to see). You can use a variety of strategies—or some combination of the tools mentioned next—to help students identify your comments.

Bold, Italics, and Other Text Emphasis Tools

Using bold, italics, underlining, or a different-colored font (for example, you could create a macro to make comments in blue), you can easily set off your comments from the rest of the text. I prefer ALL CAPS, although in the world of electronic textual discussion, this method can be (rightly) seen as a version of virtual shouting. But I like it because it's easy—just press Caps Lock and type—and your comments stand out. Also, there is no problem of translation if students use a different word processor. ALL CAPS STAND OUT ANYWHERE.

- ◆ **In-text markers.** Use an asterisk * or other character to mark all of your comments. One advantage is that students can use word processor search functions (for instance, in Word you use CTRL+F) to search through a document to find all of the comments. I used this method when writing this book, marking every place where I needed better evidence or a clearer source with * and then using CTRL+F to find those areas.

◆ **Track changes and similar word-processing functions.** Most word processors have a function that allows you to track changes you make to a document. Thus, anything you write is automatically highlighted, and deletions and notes are recorded in marginalia. You can also add comments that appear in balloons or are keyed with a hyperlink. These functions are great, although students sometimes have trouble because of technology issues: they might have difficulty seeing the changes, and if they translate the text into some other file form, those comments might be lost.

Computer Write or Highlighting Functions

Some word processors have a write or highlighting function that allows you to write on top of text or highlight text in various colors. Tablet computers can also be used in this way, and in fact, this might help you replicate the response process that you are accustomed to using: writing comments by hand for students.

End or Global Comments

Few writing teachers rely solely on in-text comments. Most of us also include some kind of comprehensive comment at either the end or the beginning of the document. If you've spent your entire career writing comments by hand on hard copies, you'll find the online environment makes you a lot happier. Your students might be a lot happier too, especially if your handwritten comments are hard to read, like mine. If they are hard to read, they might also have been tiring to write, and fatigue may in part lead to the "mean-spiritedness" scholars like Sommers have noticed in many teacher comments (149).

In the OWcourse you will receive most, if not all, of your students' writing electronically. Your global comment in these documents can simply be typed into the beginning or end of the document, perhaps as a letter. Because most of us can type more quickly than write, and with less strain, typing a decent global comment offers many advantages, one being legibility. You can also return comments to students via email, message board, or a return dropbox on your **CMS**. Each of these functions allows you to write your comment in that medium.

Creating the written global comment isn't much of a worry in the OWcourse. You can do what you normally have done, except now you can do it in an e-environment using electronic tools. Rubric creation software can be a help to you in guiding these comments, so explore those tools as well.

Voice Comments

The use of audio is nothing new in writing response, dating back at least to the 1960s (Warnock, "Responding"). At that time, teachers such as Virginia Fitzpatrick anguished over better ways to respond to their students (372). Using a cutting-edge technology for its time, they began to explore audiotaped feedback, and many followed in their footsteps over the next three decades. This approach to commenting allowed fairly localized comments to be provided on essays with the ease of voice.

Especially if you are in a true distance learning environment, you might be struck by how difficult it is to communicate with your students via writing. You might never see them or talk to them, so you might feel under significant pressure to articulate clearly what you think should be done to improve their writing. You might just like to talk to your students about their drafts. If so, this need not change with voice technologies.

Speech/Voice Recognition Technologies

Speech/voice recognition technologies, such as Dragon Naturally Speaking, continue to improve. Of course, such programs contain limits, including price and learning curve, but these technologies allow you to talk to your computer and have it record your voice as text. Some versions of these technologies are even built into your computer's operating system.

Other Voice Technologies

Many companies offer ways to maximize the use of voice and oral conversation in online classes. Horizon Wimba has an entire suite of voice-driven functions that can help you create voice message boards and can be integrated directly into your CMS. Voice-over Internet Protocol (VoIP) software such as Skype can also provide teaching alternatives. (Type *Skype teaching* into a search engine to find suggestions about using these tools in your OWcourse.)

Phone

Don't forget that you can simply ask your distance students to send you drafts electronically, and you can both open a copy of the draft while having a phone conversation about it.

Teleconferencing Technologies

As I discuss in Chapter 14, a lot of conferencing software is available, and your CMS probably will have it built in. You can set times to "meet" students in virtual spaces, talking with individuals or even groups while using various options to place the actual draft on a shared virtual workspace (or **whiteboard**).

Inserted Spoken Comments

Some programs allow you to insert voice comments. For instance, some versions of Word allow you to record comments and insert them into a document. Thomas Krucli did a good job of describing how this process works in his high school classroom (48–51). These comments can serve as audio versions of the in-text comment.

Podcasting

There are a variety of ways to incorporate voice into your teaching, and many allow you to convert the voice file into an **MP3** that students can download and listen to on their computers or handheld devices like iPods. Several universities, including the

School of Education at Drexel, have tried to encourage the use of these technologies by supplying students with free iPods or other portable devices.

Audiovisual Response

Technologies have already moved beyond voice alone. You can also easily use technologies that feature audio and video components.

Responding to Student Papers with Audiovisual Feedback

Using AV feedback (Figure 11.1) to respond to student writing in the composition classroom is still a fairly novel application, but the technologies to support this are improving at a rapid pace. I wrote a chapter detailing my use of AV technologies for the book *Writing and the iGeneration*, and I abstract that discussion here ("Responding" 205–9).

First, you need the students' writing projects in electronic form. Then you open the **screen capture** program Camtasia, follow the straightforward instructions to set up a recording, turn on the recorder, and begin—almost as if you were in a conference—talking about and typing on the paper. Any screen movement, such as highlighting blocks of text, making notations with a pen tablet, or typing text, are recorded along with the accompanying audio. Essentially, you are talking through the student's essay in a kind of virtual conference, commenting and annotating as you proceed. As you can imagine, AV feedback cranks up the response process considerably from the simple tape recorder by including a video of the paper.

In general, my students over the past few years have responded positively to this form of feedback, especially when asked to compare it to conventional written feedback. This process is much faster than evaluating papers conventionally, and I give the students more extensive feedback—saying nearly twice as much as I do in a typical written response.

Perhaps unsurprisingly, one of the biggest obstacles is the technology. You need a way to make the recordings, and then

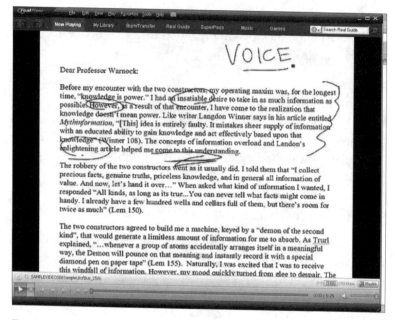

FIGURE 11.1. *View of the AV response process: the student watches as I annotate the draft and listens to my accompanying audio commentary.*

you need a way to get the file to the student. At Drexel, we have a cutting-edge media server system to solve the latter problem. The Camtasia-created video shown in Figure 11.1 was formatted automatically by our Information Resources and Technology (IRT) department. All I did was place the file in an electronic dropbox, and IRT took care of the rest. You could also load the file onto a CMS, or put the file on a CD or USB drive if you are teaching a **hybrid**. This intriguing response technology might improve the response conversation between student and teacher in many ways while, not insignificantly, reducing the amount of time teachers spend responding.

Alternative Computer Interfaces and Devices

The keyboard is still our most common interface with the computer. Many people who think about human-computer interaction (for example, Nicholas Negroponte, Neal Gershenfeld, and Ray Kurzweil) believe this will change and point out that such changes are already under way. One technology already available to us, as I mentioned earlier, is the tablet. With a tablet computer, you can write on students' papers much as you always have. The big advantage to tablets is navigation and "ease of writing." Like a pencil, you pick up a stylus, put it where you want, and write. You can save the marked-up files in several formats to deliver them to students.

I am hardly an expert in this area, but new touch-screen technologies, such as the technology that helps us interface with the iPhone, also might bring us alternative ways of responding to student writing.

I wish that, as a field, we explored our options for response more vigorously, as numerous methods of interface exist that could make our jobs easier while helping us provide better, more comprehensive feedback to our students. You can do some of those explorations on your own.

Pre-term Questions

- *How much informal writing will your students produce, and how will you respond to it?*

- *What are your deadlines for major writing projects?* Knowing this will help you structure the way you will respond and might encourage you to explore other means of response.

- *Think about ways of responding. What methods are already set up in your computer software or CMS?* Does your computer run word-processing software that allows you to highlight? To record voice? How easy is it to create macros? The technology can help you get a sense of the possibilities. Practice on older documents to determine the kind of response you want to provide. What is it like to type ALL CAPS comments? To use track changes?

- *Are you willing to try more advanced technologies? Who can help you?* If you want to try AV feedback, you'll need to have the technology set up before the term starts. Who—on campus or in the broader universe of writing instructors—can help you with that?

CHAPTER TWELVE

Grading: Should It Change When You Teach Online?

Grading and response differ. In this chapter we will look at ways that your administration of grades might change in the OW course.

I believe that your philosophy of grading a composition course should change when you teach online. As Martin Weller said, "A web-based course requires the educator to rethink his/her assessment strategy, if it is to reflect appropriately the aims of the course and assess the skills developed during the course" (110). The weighting of your course requirements should shift, if for no other reason than that some, and perhaps a significant portion, of the course grade will consist of **asynchronous**, informal electronic writing. Even if you use a lot of informal writing in your classes already, it's likely—especially if you follow the philosophy of this book—that you will use more of that material than ever when you move online.

In your onsite classes, your grading might have looked something like this:

- Three writing projects (or final writing portfolio): 45 percent (15 percent each)

- Final writing project: 25 percent

- Journal: 15 percent

- Quizzes: 10 percent

- Participation: 5 percent

If this resembles your grade scheme, then your way of thinking about the grade percentages in your class will change. If you already use a large amount of **informal writing**—especially some electronic assignments such as message boards—in the grading scheme of your onsite classes, you might have an easier time making the conceptual switch to including a chunk of this informal material in your grade.

As I have noted repeatedly, the sheer amount of writing in an online writing class opens up significant teaching and learning possibilities. Students will be writing to communicate nearly every important idea they have (and reading a great deal, too). Their informal writing should be taken seriously by everyone in the class, so you should reflect your expectations by making this writing count for a lot.

I have found that the informal assignments in my **OWcourse** —message boards, peer review, mini assignments—need to be boosted up to about 30 to 40 percent of the grade. I can easily justify this large percentage, because I ask a great deal of students in these posts (see Chapter 8 for the rules and structure of posts). Because posts are worth so much, students are compelled to take them seriously. The payoff? The writing on these boards is some of the best and, to me, the most genuine I have ever read from my writing students. Now, you may try to resist this tendency to motivate your students with grades, but I think that if we must administer grades, as most of us must, then we should accept that and work within the system as constructively as we can.

I suggest that you de-emphasize the paper/essay and participation components of your final grade (the spirit-of-participation components will be preserved in the electronic course conversations). You may find other electronic ways of replacing journals (see Chapter 9 for journal alternatives), and those materials could be included in the informal grade, or be separate.

So when the class described earlier is taught as an OWcourse, the percentage of grade might now shift to this:

- ◆ Informal writing/message boards: 35 percent

- ◆ Three writing projects (final writing portfolio): 30 percent (10 percent each)

- Final writing project: 15 percent
- Journal/**blog**: 10 percent
- Quizzes: 10 percent

This grading scheme places emphasis on your students doing some introspective or process-oriented informal writing in the form of a journal or blog. If you include that as part of the informal writing in the class, you can see how the percentages for informal writing could climb even higher.

Guideline 34: Rethink how you will weight the various components of your classes when you teach an OWcourse.

Grading Informal Writing

How exactly do you grade the regular 100- to 200-word informal pieces produced over the course of the term? There are many ways to do this (see Chapter 8), and your strategy might depend on a diverse set of influences, from how you view the power of a grade to how accomplished you are at math.

Holistic

Because students can produce a lot of written work, you might want to simplify your grading. You may find it better to use a holistic scale, perhaps each week giving students an idea of how much writing will be worth based on quality, quantity, and frequency of posting. At a presentation at the Distance Learning Association Conference in 2007, Camilla Gant of the University of West Georgia discussed a useful holistic method of grading responses that included points for analytical reflection, evidence/support, **response**, writing, and format. Students can earn a total of 100 points in these categories. For instance, the 45-point analytical reflection criterion states, "Present at least three discussion points based on a combination of premises and claims. Discussion points should advance overall understanding of subject matter." Terms such as *premises* are carefully defined on this rubric.

Grade It All

I am a glutton. I like to grade everything. Some have argued against grading posts and similar informal, computer-mediated communications. For instance, in 1991 well-known computers and composition scholars Gail Hawisher and Cynthia Selfe said that grading in this way circumvents the "positive activities" such environments produce (63–64). However, I give students a slew of grades in my online courses, and I feel that in this way, grades can be used constructively as a means of generating an ongoing conversation with students about their progress—and I stress *conversation*. Grading is too often a one-way announcement to students from the instructor. I'm struck by the fact that although I have always emphasized how much I welcome inquiries about grades, few students actually ask me to explain their grades beyond the response comments I have written. However, in the OWcourse, when you start giving students a lot of small grades, suddenly you have an opportunity to create a real conversation about their progress, because multiple small grades create an ongoing feedback mechanism.

I mentioned the use of rubrics in Chapter 11. You can use a simple rubric, even just a conceptual one, to evaluate informal writing. For instance, as described in Chapter 8, I use a ten-point scale for most informal assignments, and for response/**secondary posts** on message boards, I use a five-point scale. Conceptually, this is easy for me. An 8 is the standard grade for an informal assignment that is dutiful but not spectacular. If they crank it up, students can get a 9. More ambitious posts get a 10. Students in my classes often earn 9 and 10. Lesser efforts receive lower scores, which include factoring in lateness. (See Chapter 8 for the exact criteria.)

Quizzing

Returning to the premise of this book, teaching online isn't so much wandering into a completely new pedagogical territory as it is thinking hard about how to convert your teaching strengths from one environment to another. When I started teaching online and had to list my teaching strategies, the list included quizzing.

Although the reasons differed slightly, to me it still made sense to quiz in the OWcourse. I use reading quizzes to start most of my onsite classes, and I have maintained that frequent quizzing practice online (backed by the philosophy that easy, fun quizzes help students structure their reading), but I decrease the weight of the quizzes so I don't spend too much time policing students and trying to create cheat-free quizzes. (The following material connects with information in Chapter 7, where I discussed reading.)

I don't quiz because I am mean. No, I think quizzing is one of the most effective ways to help my students read more closely, and I described my approach and philosophy in an article I wrote for the *Teaching Professor*, "Quizzes Boost Comprehension, Confidence" (1). My initial title also included the phrase *conversation and community*. I see the humble start-of-class reading quiz as an effective pedagogical tool to begin class with energy and a positive vibe, and to help students read the material—and feel good about their understanding of it. It's important to add this: my reading quizzes are ridiculously easy.

Whether online or onsite, I still quiz to encourage students to read; and they want to do well on these simple quizzes. Although Michael Marcell focused on the use of online quizzing for onsite classes, his finding that quizzes led students to ask better reading-related questions in class is relevant for us. He also found that students were more likely to complete the readings, and that students "reported that regular quizzing provided a structure for studying that encouraged them to pace their reading and to work harder to understand the material" (2). The five-minute time limit I use makes it unlikely that students will succeed on a quiz going into it cold. They just don't have enough time to browse through the readings while taking the quiz. Like Marcell, I also use quizzing to establish a sense of *pacing*. In f2f classes, I begin class with a quiz so students are on time and the class opening has a familiar feel: Class starts . . . now! The situation is different online, but pacing is even more important (see Chapter 13). Students, in this virtual environment, should learn to expect X to happen on Wednesdays, Y to happen on Thursdays, and so on. Quizzes are a great tool for this. On the same day throughout the term, I open my quizzes from 9:30 a.m. to a little after midnight (a 12:00 a.m. deadline gets you into trouble—too much room for error in describing when midnight falls).

In the online environment, I still want the quizzes to be easy so students feel good about what they are doing. This is the kind of question I ask: "What happens to Romeo at the end of *Romeo and Juliet?*" There is little in the way of analysis here; I just want them to read. If they say something about Romeo's triumphant lap around Verona, then I know they haven't read the whole work.

Teachers might wonder how to administer a quiz online. My quizzes are easy, so I simply give students five minutes to complete them; it would be harder and more time-consuming to cheat on the quiz than just to take the darn thing. If you are worried about students taking the quiz together, you can complicate matters by using **question set**s, a simple feature in most any **CMS**. For a five-question quiz, say you create ten questions. The software then randomly chooses five questions for each student, thus creating a different quiz for everyone in the class (Figure 12.1).

Finally, the online and onsite quizzes share another key feature of my quizzing strategy: low stakes. Students can drop a quiz or two. I'm not trying to corner my students or frustrate them—with one possible outcome being that they cheat, which means we all lose. Instead, I try to give them a constructive, easy, rewarding

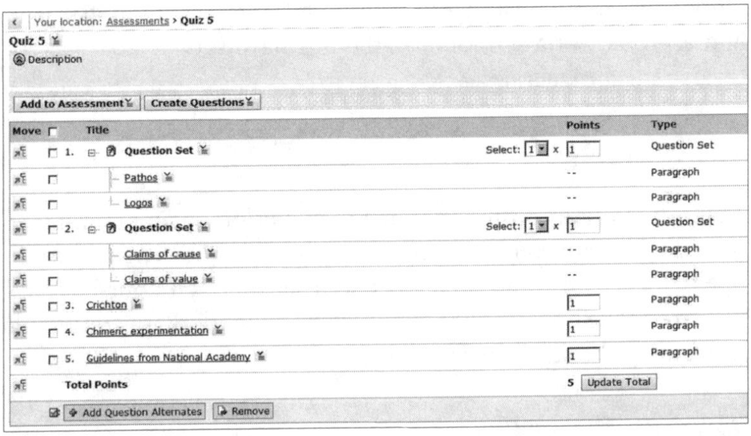

FIGURE **12.1.** *Example of question sets on a quiz. Questions 1 and 2 have two options from which the quiz program will randomly select one question for each quiz taker.*

method to demonstrate their learning. Soon enough, we will build on that learning in the higher-stakes assignments in the course.

Tests

Although biometric authentication might soon solve some of these problems (Ko and Rossen 252), right now administering high-stakes tests to fully online students is an imprecise science. As Ko and Rossen pointed out, "For many instructors, the prospect of online testing may raise the issue of plagiarism. How do you know which student is taking a test if it's taken online?" (251). I have not administered tests to students in my online writing classes, and in fact, one of the strengths of the OWcourse compared with other environments is that we have a great many assessment opportunities to familiarize ourselves with our students through their writing. Every CMS has a way to administer tests; the issue seems to be more about student identity.

Proctored Exams

If you want to administer tests, you might be able to assemble your students in a room proctored by you or someone else. For schools with true distance learners, students are often asked to find a proctor at a school near them (I have served as a proctor for distance learners).

Timed Exams

You can also administer tests in a fixed period of time, similar to the way I administer five-minute reading quizzes. The test could open at a set time and then close at a set time. Of course, you'll need to decide how much is enough time to work on the test while restraining the students from dishonesty.

The Take-Home Test

Sometimes I think we make things too complicated. Take-home tests are a trusted tool in many teaching situations, so consider administering them to your OWcourse students in much the same way as in an onsite course. The test could open at a certain time, and then students would have a day or so to work on the material. Of course, such tests are often complex enough to warrant such out-of-class time, but remember that *everyone is working under the same constraints*, and it is from such balanced test administration that fairness emanates.

Grading Major Writing Projects

This chapter has addressed methods of approaching and grading smaller assignments. As I mentioned in Chapter 11, your handling of larger written projects might not change much when you move into the online environment, especially if you have become accustomed to receiving and replying to papers electronically. Much of what I would say about grading these larger projects is covered in Chapter 11.

One area of grading projects that I believe is worth noting: unless you are using voice technologies, remember that you are relying heavily on the written word to respond to students. We don't have the visual cues—the blank stares, for instance—of the onsite class, so we need to build these types of "feedback mechanisms" into our online class (Smith 35). Be as clear as possible in your written comments, and keep in mind that student writers who are struggling in your class might have reading issues—or apathy issues—that prevent them from reading well or closely. You'll need to strike the classic balance in grading major projects, touching on areas of improvement without overwhelming the student with your comments. There are many composition sources to help you with that task (see Chapter 18).

Making Grades Available to Students

Another aspect of the OWcourse that might carry over to your onsite teaching is the use of a course gradebook. Any CMS has some form of gradebook, and this tool can help you present students with all of their grades in an easy, streamlined way. Especially if you are giving a lot of grades in the course, you'll want a grading solution like this for your students. Surely we don't want students to be unaware of their grades as the term progresses. The gradebook also provides a check system so students can make sure you have recorded all of their grades. I might give more than 1,300 grades in a term to one class, so I am bound to make a mistake. I'm glad to have students check the grades for me.

Pre-term Questions

♦ *Have you thought through the weighting of your grade scale, accounting for the additional writing students will do online?*

♦ *Is there anything different you would like to incorporate into the students' major and minor writing grades in the course?* You could develop a rubric for either or both of these components of your course.

♦ *Do you think you will use quizzes or exams in your course?* If so, you'll want to see how to administer these tools via your CMS.

CHAPTER THIRTEEN

Pacing and Predictability: Help Students Get Comfortable in the OWcourse

Because students in an OWcourse do not have the built-in structure of attending class every two or three days, you should create repetitive, predictable deadlines to help them feel anchored to the weekly work in the course.

Teachers must create a sense of pacing and predictability in an online class. Students are creatures of habit. Reflect for a moment: in your onsite classes, after throwing off the shackles of assigned seating from middle and high school, your students still sit in the same seats every class. In fact, they get annoyed if someone takes "their" spot (I think there was a study that even verified this). In addition, the lack of **f2f** time in an online class can be a danger for some students. They don't have to go to class several times a week, so they may allow course work to slide away . . . and then find themselves in trouble. Use simple strategies and tools to pace the class and give a sense of structure and consistency so students can get into the work flow and spend their main energies trying to succeed academically.

Guideline 35: Create a structure of deadlines and predictable elements for your class so that students become comfortable with the course schedule.

Posted Schedule and Course Work Plans

As I discussed in Chapter 6, I use a **Weekly Plan** approach in my class. In my plan, I describe what is due using a three-column HTML document with the following column headings:

- ◆ What do I do?

- ◆ What are the specific instructions? Where do I find the work or the assignment?

- ◆ When is it due?

I normally post the plan for the following week on Thursday afternoon or Friday morning. If I'm late, I let the students know by posting an explanation on the homepage. See the Teaching Materials Appendix for an example of a Weekly Plan.

Message Board Deadlines

I use a two-tiered deadline system for my message board conversations. Since I post the Weekly Plan on Fridays, I use a Wednesday-Friday deadline for posts (I once used Thursday-Saturday, but I don't work much on Saturdays, so I had trouble getting involved with the later discussions). On Wednesday, several **primary posts** are due. On Friday, **secondary post**s are due. I ask students if these deadlines are okay. If so, I stick with them so students get accustomed to when they are responsible for these core class conversations. I would be flexible with the deadlines if another schedule worked better for students.

Quizzes

Following up on the discussion in Chapter 12, there is more to quizzes than just encouraging students to read or measuring their comprehension in other areas. A weekly or biweekly quiz, even a ridiculously easy reading quiz, can be a mighty aid in helping students have a sense of consistency in the weekly structure of the course. I give my quizzes on the same day all term, and students say that they soon become accustomed to this routine.

Mini and Informal Assignments

I think it's a mistake in any writing class not to use a series of very small (each worth about 1 percent of the grade) assignments. Have students describe what they are attempting to do in each paragraph of their essays. Ask them to take a piece of writing and try to change all instances of the verb *to be*. Ask them to pick their best message board posts and comment on them. These informal *metawriting* assignments are valuable for students' development, but they also fill in the gaps between message board posts and the main assignments. They create a dutiful sense of work flow in the class—and you shouldn't feel you have to grade them with more than a glance.

Videos and Multimedia Lessons

In addition to the other benefits, creating a video or audio of yourself every other week can help lock students back into the idea that you are a real teacher "out there." Linking a video to an informal assignment or message board post helps encourage them to watch these lessons, and it helps the pacing during the rough draft/final draft cycle.

A typical schedule for my **OWcourse** might look like this:

- Friday: Weekly Plan posted
- Tuesday: Informal assignment due or deadline to watch video
- Wednesday: Deadline for readings so students can be ready for the quiz and message boards
- Wednesday: Reading quiz (available for eighteen hours); primary message board posts due
- Friday: Secondary message board posts due; weblog entry due

It's a rough analogy, but I think that not having a consistent set of deadlines is like asking students to attend an onsite course in which they never know the meeting time until the class before. Obviously, this would be maddening. Keep them focused on small, low-stakes deadlines, and they will be less likely to put off their online class work—and they'll have a better chance of succeeding.

Pre-term Questions

- *When is the best time to have reading deadlines?* Many other aspects of the class will follow from your reading deadlines.

- *What techniques will you use to keep students informed of what is due each week?* This is crucial. I use a Weekly Plan, so students are not scurrying all over our **CMS** site looking for their work each week.

- *Do you have the ability to make short videos?* Consult your local technical staff to learn your options for creating short, simple videos that might help keep your students plugged into your role as a "real" teacher.

- *Can you create a set of consistent activity dates in the class?* If so, you will help your students with the kind of pacing I described in this chapter.

CHAPTER FOURTEEN

Collaboration: Working
in Virtual Groups

Teaching writing online does not mean the end of collaborative learning. Many techniques and tools can help you assign teamwork in the OWcourse.

One concern teachers express to me about teaching writing online is that the collaborative aspects of their teaching will be lost. For many of us, collaboration is vital. Your online writing class can still have a great deal of collaboration; and again highlighting an advantage of the **OWcourse**, that collaboration can focus closely on texts and be driven by students' *writing* instead of speaking skills. Even if you are getting comfortable with the technology, you might feel uncertain about employing it for collaboration in online settings. David Brandon and Andrea Hollingshead argued strongly for using "collaborative-learning concepts" online because of three trends: (1) "the widespread interest in organizational learning," (2) the common use of communication technologies, and (3) "the ubiquitous presence of groups in modern organizations" (285). In other words, people all over the world are collaborating in this way—why not your students?

Most **CMS** packages have functions that allow you to place students into teams; some even create the teams randomly. Then you can associate certain tools with a given team of students, such as a chat room, a **whiteboard**, and a message board **thread** that only that team can see. With these simple tools, you can use a number of collaborative activities and projects in your online writing class.

> **Guideline 36**: You can use collaborative assignments in many ways in your OWcourse, so you don't have to abandon group projects online.

Team Projects

Much as you can with the typical lengthy individual writing assignments in your onsite classes, in your move to the OWcourse, you can preserve the kinds of collaborative assignments that have worked for you in the past. I second Bender's advice that the groups be small, no bigger than four or five people (119).

One team assignment I have used with success is to have students collaborate to create an argument website. I continue to be pleasantly surprised—and sometimes amazed—at the work that my student teams have done almost strictly through electronic collaboration. As long as the assignment and the students' objectives are clear, they can do excellent work together in the e-environment, using various technology tools to communicate.

Although they email each other and use their phones and **IM** functions to communicate, I often ask that they also use the CMS message board so I can be part of their conversations and troubleshoot when things go wrong; this openness helps me avoid any Big Brother issues (Bender 119). And things do go wrong, as with most collaborative projects. However, I have noticed a slightly greater tendency toward nonparticipation in online group projects. I try to be heavily involved when I see this happening, but some students seem to willfully ignore messages from the team until it's too late. You must be extra vigilant to make sure students don't drift away. The technology could be to blame, but Brandon and Hollingshead also considered it a potential advantage: although communication technology "may add to the complexity of the learning tasks," it encourages learning about the technology itself, which can promote cooperation in groups (289). Students might adopt a we're-all-in-this-together attitude and work closely to help each other. Brandon and Hollingshead also pointed out that technology will always influence a "group's progress to some degree," but that technology is "ultimately less influential than the overall instructional strategy" (305).

Student Roles

I emphasize that my students create clear roles in group projects, and I *really* emphasize that in the OWcourse. Students can take roles such as leader, meeting organizer, secretary, head researcher, chief editor (they all should, of course, participate in the research and editing of a project), Web designer, and so on. They should be clear about their responsibilities each week, and I find it helpful to take part occasionally, checking in to make sure these activities are completed. It's especially helpful to identify a clear group leader with whom I can talk to get progress updates about the group; often, I end up talking to that person on the phone at some point to address an issue the group is having.

Peer Review

We talked about peer review in several previous chapters, so I won't belabor the point here. You can place students into three- to five-person groups and have virtual writing workshops. Ask every student to start a thread by attaching (or cutting and pasting) their project to a post. Then ask them, using specific questions or guidelines, to critique each paper. Require them to account for previous posts in their critiques so you won't get the same responses over and over and so a workshop-style environment can develop. You can even ask students to respond to their review posts. You might decide to keep the same peer review teams together all term.

Message Board Subgroups

Many onsite teachers like to start general class conversations by having groups of students team up and discuss specific aspects of a reading or topic before convening as a class. This helps students

talk and think in a more close-knit, and possibly less intimidating, environment. You can create the same dynamic on message
boards by having small breakout groups—again, set up by your
CMS and accessible only to members of that group—focus on
a particular aspect of a topic before having a general conversation with the whole group. If you find your message boards are
flat, you might also use this method to encourage students to be
more conversationally assertive. Students sometimes are able to
talk more comfortably when there are only a few people in the
initial audience.

You can also use subgroups if you want everyone to comment on a topic or lesson, but you don't think there is enough to
say for the whole class. For instance, sometimes I have students
look through a reading for logical fallacies (see Chapter 9). I want
them to post their findings on a message board, but there are not
enough passages for the whole class. If you break students into
groups, each group can tackle the assignment fresh.

Synchronous Communications

Lots of tools—both freestanding and within the CMS—can provide whiteboards on which groups of students can work, chat
areas, and even voice conferencing arrangements. All of this
was mentioned in previous chapters, and you don't need to get
complicated: explore your CMS and see what's available. Having
students work together on a whiteboard or even participate in a
chat moderated by you—which will be different from the casual
chatting they are used to—can help them see how an idea can
develop based on collective writing.

More than twenty years ago, Bruffee wrote, "Knowledge is the
product of human beings in a state of continual negotiation or
conversation" (1), helping frame a model of composition teaching
that embraced collaboration. In some ways this was a hard-fought
battle, one that we still fight today when faced with conceptions
of plagiarism that ignore the fact that writing, thinking, and *being* are collaborative endeavors (for instance, Candace Spigelman
discussed how writing groups complicate the academy's concepts

of plagiarism and textual ownership). We do not want to lose the essence of that teaching philosophy when we teach online, and there is no reason that we should.

Pre-term Questions

- ◆ *Do you use team assignments in your onsite classes?* If so, think about how they might migrate to the online environment.

- ◆ *How does the team/group function work in your CMS?* Consult your local technical staff if you are unsure, but these functions are normally straightforward.

- ◆ *Do you want students to work together, and do you have assignments that allow for this?*

CHAPTER FIFTEEN

Intellectual Property: Plagiarism, Copyright, and Trust

According to many sources, a lot of cheating takes place in American schools of higher education. In this chapter I explain how the OWcourse can provide a number of constructive obstacles to plagiarism. And because teachers and students might have the same kinds of questions about intellectual property, I also briefly discuss issues of copyright.

Plagiarism

In my design for this book, I hesitated to include a chapter on plagiarism. As reviewers noted—and I agreed—it just seems so, well, *negative*. But in my defense, my concept of myself as teacher does *not* involve policing my students. I trust them, and my goal is to work closely with them to help them develop and improve their writing. This goal comes across consistently on my student evaluations—even in the midst of critiques of my tough grading! I also believe, in line with many who have written thoughtfully about plagiarism, that the best ways to guard against plagiarism are through intelligent, creative assignment design and by close attention to students' process and revision of work (see Rebecca Moore Howard, "Forget").

New technologies, however, have changed the plagiarism landscape and the way we think about plagiarism. "New technologies . . . continue to keep concerns surrounding plagiarism in the forefront of the collective academic psyche," wrote English Professor James Purdy. "If plagiarism is easier to commit because of the Internet, it is also easier to catch because of the Internet. We in English studies must, therefore, now think about plagiarism in light of technology" (275–76). Despite how much we want to trust and believe in our students, we cannot be ignorant of the many studies indicating that students cheat (see Jill Austin and Linda Brown, Suzy Hansen, or Sadie Williams, all of whom cite evidence about student cheating). Many others plagiarize in ways that are not overtly cheating, perhaps in line with the more subtle cases on Howard's plagiarism continuum, on which the most obvious cases are classified as "fraud" and the others make up a range of lesser offenses, often because the students do not understand what they can borrow and how to do it ("Sexuality" 475). The bottom line is that we must consider that students might cheat in our **OWcourse**s, and this is an extension of the broader "possibility of fraud and cheating" (Ko and Rossen 60) in any online instructional environment.

However, I think the OWcourse can help us thwart plagiarism. After all, we read so much more of our students' writing in online courses, so that familiarity we develop with their writing increases. Weller noted that the frequent interaction between instructors and students creates an environment that obstructs plagiarism (115), and Bender said, "Because of frequently reading student responses throughout the semester, any written reports or essays should not come as a surprise in terms of credibility and authenticity" (148). I think that the online writing environment can actually help lessen students' tendency to plagiarize, and, in an interesting twist, it can enlist a whole class full of invested participants to help maintain a culture of honesty and openness in your class. This is one more positive side effect to the massive sharing of texts in the OWcourse.

Guideline 37: The inherent openness of the OWcourse can help you curb plagiarism constructively, putting it in the backseat of your concerns, where it belongs.

The best guard against plagiarism is to use a process approach with focused, course-specific assignments. Let's face it: if you assign students to write a three-page paper about Hamlet's indecisiveness, you are practically challenging some of them to plagiarize. And not to defend the cheaters, but our students well understand the difference between a writing assignment that represents authentic communication between you and them and a hoop you are making them jump through.

When I feel the euphoria of reading a strong effort from one of my students, I don't immediately fall into suspicious mode. But I also know that I need to create an environment of reasonable obstacles to discourage cheating and help support the efforts of the vast majority of students who are doing their own work. The text-heavy environment of the OWcourse does a great deal to help that.

Using Student Texts

In the OWcourse, you are not the only one who has the chance to read many of your students' texts: they will read each other's all term. You can use this inherent trait of teaching writing online to erect further barriers to inauthentic student documents. However, remember that the OWcourse is in some ways a massive, ongoing peer review of student text sharing. Hewett and Ehmann described the pressure that this can put on students, who aren't always sure what they can borrow and what they can't when they work in collaborative environments (49–51). But because so much of their texts are in the public of class, this too can be a topic of open discussion in your OWcourse.

Knowing Your Students, Knowing Their Texts

After reading two or three projects by our students—and sometimes fewer (the kind of *thin slicing* that Malcolm Gladwell described in *Blink*)—we begin to become aware of their style and method as writers. Now, imagine that on top of the formal writing, you are also reading thousands of words of **informal writing**. That is one big advantage of the OWcourse, and I can't minimize its importance in terms of plagiarism: you will have so much evidence about their writing that you will have a strong intuitive judgment about what is theirs and what is not. You will develop an intimacy with your students' writing that is difficult to match in onsite courses, because such a large part of their class work ends up in written form. Even a series of emails can offer you insight into a student's writing persona.

Public Drafts

A student can try to slip one by you and might succeed, even in a process-oriented class. But in an online class, writing is consistently in a semipublic space. More eyes than yours will be on that document, so there are multiple opportunities for other students to gain familiarity with their colleagues' texts, even beyond the normal peer review in your onsite course.

This familiarity can grow out of the frequent use of informal writing spaces such as message boards, **wikis**, and **blogs**. In fact, I once had two students "out" another student who plagiarized a message board post in the public space of the class. In explaining how he came to the discovery, one student said, "It seemed unlike any post I had seen from the author. In an online class, you begin to find the common writing styles of your peers. When the author showed a completely different writing style, I had a feeling the post was plagiarized" (Warnock, "Awesome" 183). The students were able, through the process of having reviewed and read each other's materials, to discern stylistic differences leading them to a simple Google search that uncovered a colleague's plagiarism. After several weeks, students begin to get a feel for each other's written communications, and they, as well as you, can pick up on drastic differences in the style and content of their classmates' posts.

Students as Sources

One technique you might also try is to require students to use each other's posts as sources. This requirement is a great benefit of the online writing class, and has various conceptual advantages, including that it is a layer of protection against plagiarism: even students who buy a project from an online paper mill must find a way to include several quotes from their classmates. I have uncovered some cases of plagiarism by finding disjunctures in projects that included in-class student quotes; nothing in the papers, except the student quotes, sounded like it belonged in the context of our class.

Using Electronic Plagiarism Detection Tools

Online plagiarism detection tools, Turnitin specifically, have been embroiled in many disputes. Student objections have included that the software violates student copyright in order to do its job (Arnoldy). Teacher objections have included that the software creates antagonistic relationships between teacher and student. Institutions might decry the cost of software that can create the problems that students and teachers find.

I think that online plagiarism tools have their place in our teaching world and that we should take advantage of them. You can use these tools any way you like, and I believe you can use them in a way that creates a constructive classroom environment that legitimately protects the majority of good students from the sins of the few. The originality checker Turnitin (Figure 15.1) can be configured so students can see the *originality report* that

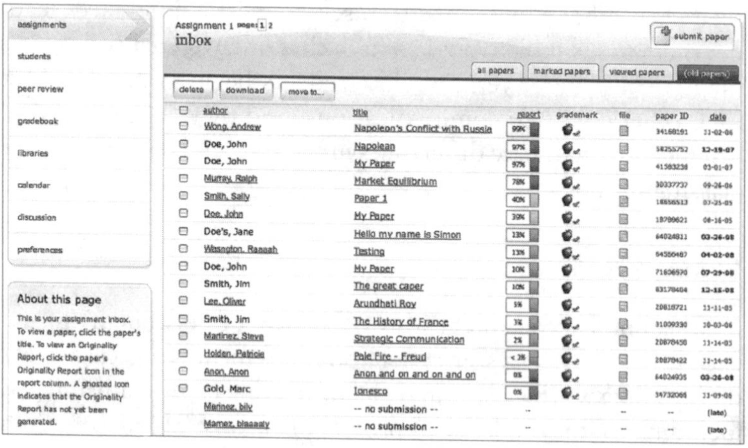

FIGURE 15.1. *View of Turnitin's submission page (with fake student names), including originality reports. (Thanks to Turnitin for providing this image.)*

is generated and then resubmit the project, using the originality problems marked by the software to improve their ability to cite.

In fact, these originality reports—which can pick up quotes, regardless of whether they are cited correctly—can help students see when too little or too much of their written project relies on directly quoted material. Even when we suspect plagiarism, our approach need not be aggressive or hostile. As Dànielle DeVoss and Annette Rosati noted, students often do not *know* they have plagiarized: "Rather than approach plagiarism as an affront to our values and authority as teachers, issues of plagiarism can provide a scaffolding for discussions relating to appropriate research, good writing, similarities and differences in research spaces, intellectual property rights, and the pitfalls and potentials of electronic media" (201). We can turn plagiarism conversations into constructive teaching moments.

The main plagiarist I want to check is the lazy student who buys a paper and slaps it up as his or her own, or, worse, who steals a roommate's efforts. Turnitin, though imperfect, can protect against those sorts of transgressions, especially if everyone in your program is on board with it. Remember that in an OW-course, many student documents are electronically available on the Web. In fact, you can even run into cases of multiple copying of the same document, unfortunately transforming you into a detective who must determine where and when a document was first created and who subsequently copied it. Technology tools have their place, but they should not supplant good teaching practices. Purdy said that thinking about the connection between technology and plagiarism can help us from panicking about rampant plagiarism; we need "to consider the role the writing technologies [students] use play in their writing processes and consider how we as teachers . . . can pedagogically address these technologies." Our job, he suggested, is to focus on connections between plagiarism and technology, and to remember our role as *teacher* so we spend our time educating students about plagiarism rather than "at the computer testing student papers for unattributed language" (291).

As an aside, I also like Turnitin's document dropbox feature. It makes bulk download of all student documents fast, easy, and straightforward.

Search Engines

Of course, you can use search engines such as Google or Yahoo! to do your own version of what Turnitin does automatically. Writing teachers are good at picking up the cadences, syntax, and diction of our students' writing. If something seems amiss, you can put the power of these search engines to use by typing in a phrase within quotation marks. Using quotation marks limits the search to exact phrases. This is a quick and easy way to check a suspect passage.

Metadata

Here is a simple way to detect plagiarism. Remember that when most word-processing documents are created, they have accompanying **metadata** in the file, which tell you when and on what computer the file was created (Figure 15.2). This could help you find the smoking gun on a contested paper that two (or more) students have handed in.

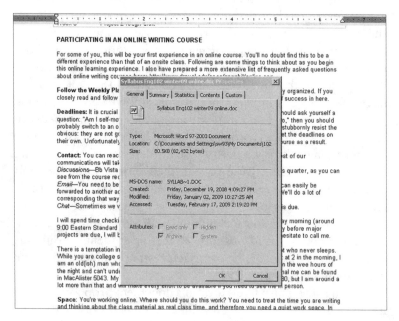

FIGURE 15.2. *Example of the metadata that accompany Word documents.*

Stakes

My final comment about avoiding plagiarism is not exclusive to the online writing environment. It seems that students are likely to cheat more when the stakes are high. Only a few high-counting tests or written projects push students to make the most of these opportunities; and "making the most of it" is interpreted by some students as a rationalization for cheating, as Audrey Amrein and David Berliner of Arizona State University discovered in a study of high-stakes testing.

As I have mentioned, although my focus is on teaching writing online, many e-learning pedagogies also translate well to onsite teaching. For example, if you create more grading opportunities, you create more spaces for students to experiment and take risks. If you find ways to make more grades available to your students, that might reduce their temptation to hand in work that is not their own.

> **Guideline 38:** The vast majority of your students will not plagiarize egregiously in your OWcourse, but it's your obligation to try to catch those who do.

Copyright: Speaking of Complex Webs . . .

The rules and guidelines for copyright are dense and tricky. More than a decade ago, CONFU (Conference on Fair Use) attempted to hammer out rules and guidelines to help educators navigate the difficult waters of copyright. Ko and Rossen's "simple answer" about the guidelines for copyright for online educators takes this form: "Copyright law, as it is written, states that if you're using material that belongs to others without their permission and the material you're using is freely accessible . . . then you're probably breaking the law and thus vulnerable to a suit by the material's rightful owner" (166).

> **Guideline 39**: Copyright is complex. If you are using borrowed materials, you will want to consult *several* sources, starting with your local librarian, to understand the range and limitations of fair use.

It's tempting to use materials for your class at will, especially if you are working in the private space of a password-protected **CMS**. But be wary: although the authors of *Code of Best Practices in Fair Use for Media Literacy Education* say they are unaware of any lawsuits by companies against educators "over the use of media in the education process" (Center for Social Media, screen 18), if we are trying to build an environment of honesty in the course—which most of us are—we are hypocritical if we flout copyright. Observant students will notice this hypocrisy, and they may see the double standard as an invitation to break the rules. Again, I don't want to indicate that they are not to blame for their own plagiarism, but it would be a shame if that plagiarism were encouraged by our own sloppy copyright practices. I once attended a copyright seminar at Temple University, and I remember the feeling of discomfort that crept over the room as we all learned what constitutes copyright violation. All of the participants seemed upset, perhaps because they had been in the dark about this topic.

Nevertheless, you should know that there are some exceptions to copyright, especially when materials are used for educational purposes. These exceptions fall loosely under the concept of *fair use*, which for our purposes means allowable exceptions for educators to use materials. Ko and Rossen referred to a document called *Fair Use Guidelines for Educational Multimedia* that has laid out a few exceptions for educators, revolving around four primary factors:

1. **If the work is used for commercial or noncommercial purposes.** Fair use guidelines generally state that noncommercial use of works—and much teaching falls under this—is considered much more permissible than commercial use.

2. **The nature of the work.** If the nature of the work is more creative, it is often more protected by copyright than if the work is "strictly factual" in nature. Works that are in the public domain—according to Ko and Rossen, those that are "out of copyright or never copyrighted"—are fine for a teacher to use.

3. **The amount of a work used.** Smaller amounts of a work qualify more for fair use than large amounts/large percentages. There are no exact guidelines about amount of usage—the CONFU site uses terms such as "sparingly" (CONFU)—but this criterion serves as a general rule.

4. **The effect of the use on the work's market value.** If the use would damage the work's market value, then fair use would be violated. Online educators operating their courses in a publicly accessible space should consider the accessibility of materials when making this determination. (Ko and Rossen 167–68)

Much more detail about this can be found at the *CONFU: The Conference on Fair Use* documentation on the Web, and an even more recent set of guidelines is the *Code of Best Practices in Fair Use for Media Literacy Education*. As you teach an OWcourse, keep in mind that copyright guidelines are not limited to specific technologies (Lehman 62).

Ultimately, in your search for copyright guidelines, you have allies in your own campus library staff. And more directly, Ko and Rossen have suggested that if you are unsure about copyright, take the simple step of writing a letter to the material's owner to ask for permission, with the understanding that at times, tracking down the legitimate owner of a document can be a problem (170–71). Still, this is a proactive approach you can take to figure out who owns something and to learn the parameters of that ownership.

Of necessity, this has been a brief and incomplete primer on copyright. Interestingly, many of the sources I have reviewed about teaching online include no mention of copyright. That doesn't mean you should treat copyright lightly; but if you approach the use of others' materials with a sense of fairness, and if before the term starts you are willing to take time to investigate potential violations in consultation with legal and information experts on campus, you can avoid a troublesome issue.

Pre-term Questions

- *Do your assignments invite plagiarism?* If so, how might you embed them better in your particular course context to avoid issues of plagiarism? How can assignments be creatively specific to your course?

- *What plagiarism detection software—if any—is available through your campus?* See if you can experiment with the software. Do you like what it does? Does it help reinforce the kind of message you want to give your students?

- *Are you using any readings or materials that might violate copyright?*

- *Who is the point person in your library who understands copyright?* Librarians are trained to understand these issues, and I have yet to find one who was not a willing partner in helping me design readings for my course.

CHAPTER SIXTEEN

Virtual Teaching Circles: Leveraging Teacher Time and Effort

The online environment is conducive to teacher collabo-
ration, as teams of teachers can design general course
materials that can be tailored for individual sections, and
they can communicate course lessons and strategies easily.
This chapter offers a brief look at how instructor collabo-
ration can work in the online instructional environment.

Compositionist Stephen North, writing about the history of
composition, described the repository of practitioner knowledge about composition instruction with the metaphor of the
House of Lore, "a rambling, to my mind delightful old manse"
(27). This is a charming image, but what it describes is hardly ideal
in terms of the practicality of teaching composition. Too many
good teaching ideas are buried in the dusty corners and closets
of this structure; too often teachers reinvent ideas that have been
around for years, sometimes within their own programs.

It is a nettlesome problem, this mission to unify in a handy
place the lore and skills of composition. At the end of this book,
I offer some resources to help teachers of writing do their jobs
more effectively, but as I have noted repeatedly in arguing *why*
we should consider the move to online instruction, training is
yet another area that the digitization of writing instruction can
help. Many composition programs have ways to help faculty
share ideas via websites, in-house publications, teaching circles,
and mentorship programs. Education, and writing instruction in
particular, is dynamic: people are inventing new ways daily to
help students learn. The online writing environment offers a keen
edge in this way. Through the use of the actual materials, we can

share resources among members of a department, school, or even the whole profession, leveraging technology while saving costs by the use of what Marsh, McFadden, and Price called **reusable learning objects (RLO)**. Ideally, a database of RLO could be

> shared and easily reused to generate a course of instruction according to standards adopted under the "Sharable Content Object Reference Model" (**SCORM**) and accessed by means of a Learning Management System (LMS). . . . Developing a repository of content that can be used now and in the future will save time, money, and effort by replacing lectures and reducing course preparation, a truly capital-intensive strategy . . . . By tying electronic instructional units to tests and activities, a comprehensive body of courseware could be developed that would be serviceable with little maintenance for many semesters to come. (Marsh et al., screen 9)

Accompanying this idea is the threat that teachers might be supplanted on a large scale by technology. This is a legitimate threat, but I argue that as long as we center our classes around the texts of our students and our **response** to those texts—which differs from just grading—no one is better positioned than the composition instructor to be empowered in online learning environments. We can create learning objects, but no one can evaluate student responses to those objects as we can. This is a key reason that we should be in the vanguard of teachers working in online instruction.

Shared Spaces, Shared Assignments

One obvious way to leverage technology is through the use of teaching modules, which can appear in various forms (Figure 16.1). In Chapter 9 I described several modules that can be exactly recreated and distributed to others. We simply need a shared space to do so. There are great Web models of this: for instance, MERLOT (Multimedia Educational Resources for Learning and Online Teaching). Or instructors all can be participants in a **CMS** "course" that allows them to share materials and transfer modules easily into their classes. Naturally, they must still conduct, analyze, and respond to the written work that such modules inspire, but the beauty of modules is that their ease of setup allows us to spend more time engaged in the valuable task of response.

Even if you do not use some type of shared Web space, you can distribute your assignments electronically through a variety of other means. That's the upside of digital reproducibility: rather than have a water-cooler discussion about a favorite assignment, you can send the actual assignment to other instructors.

Virtual Conversational Spaces

Teaching circles are an excellent idea, but they pose several logistical problems, especially for those who teach four or more courses a term, which is fairly standard for teaching-only faculty at many institutions. Simply getting a group of teaching faculty together can be almost impossible, as their schedules are filled with teaching commitments. In online situations, faculty may not even be in the same time zone.

Because faculty who teach online are accustomed to the tools of online instruction, it's a natural to ask them to form a virtual teaching circle using an available message board, **blog, wiki** space, or **listserv** (Figure 16.1). To encourage dialogue, you may need to accompany such spaces with a requirement that people post

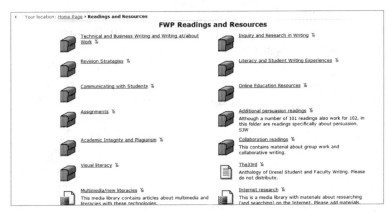

FIGURE 16.1. *The teaching resources Blackboard Vista site for Drexel's First-Year Writing Program.*

a certain number of messages so there is an actual conversation. In 2008 at Drexel, we started a discussion listserv for our sixty-plus faculty, but it was seldom used. In addition to using your CMS as a site for materials, you can also use the communication technologies available in those packages to have an ongoing teaching dialogue during the term. How the space is moderated is a decision you make.

Much as you use group functions for students, you can place teachers into smaller groups within the larger message board, thus creating a virtual teaching circle.

Web Seminars and Other E-Presentations

Those interested in technology have many options to attend Web seminars and other information presentations online. As part of a program, different teachers could offer such Web seminars, using straightforward video technology to distribute the information to faculty.

> **Guideline 40:** One composition teacher is good. A group of composition teachers sharing materials electronically is great.

As I mentioned earlier, I think we don't do enough to systematize our old "manse" of teaching instruction to draw from older materials in creating our own lessons and modules. And some reports indicate that less than 30 percent of full-time faculty who teach online receive detailed training about how to do so, and the numbers must be lower for part-timers (Henderson and Nash v). We need to create ways—at all levels, including the disciplinary and institutional—to share our resources as teachers so as to maximize the *best practices* of instruction and to refine our own approaches. In *Learning Organization*, Tim Kilby wrote, "The best designs come only after a concerted study of multiple resources. Learn from others but define your own direction" (197).

Pre-term Questions

◆ *Does your program have in place teaching circles, virtual or otherwise?*

◆ *Is there an electronic space—a web page, a shared drive—you can use to upload and share materials?*

◆ *Is there an e-space or listserv—perhaps as part of the e-space above—that allows conversation among the different teachers in your program?* If there is, you will want to think of ways to encourage participation.

CHAPTER SEVENTEEN

Course Assessment: Taking Steps toward Knowing How Well We Are Doing

This book is designed for the beginning online writing instructor, so it's premature to discuss course or programmatic assessment. But it is important for us, especially as teachers of OW courses, to always consider the effectiveness of what we are doing.

Writing teachers should think about assessment, and that goes double for online writing teachers. By *assessment*, I don't mean evaluation of students and their work. I mean assessment of our courses and, perhaps, our programs: How effective are instructional methods for writing in the online setting? What methods emerge as best practices? Is student writing different online? How? If we believe our methods are solid, and I certainly do; if we believe that the opportunities in online teaching are substantial; if we believe that we can help our students learn to write effectively—then we need to be mindful of mining the resources, textual and otherwise, at our fingertips to demonstrate that what we do online makes sense and is pedagogically sound.

> **Guideline 41:** There are numerous ways to assess what we are doing in our courses, in particular drawing on the vast number of texts that not only our students create but that we create.

Many methods, some of them relatively untapped, exist to help us demonstrate what is happening in our classes and how we might measure how student behaviors affect learning. Of course, we can look at student evaluations or surveys, but in terms of assessment efforts, I believe that far too much emphasis is already placed on these tools. There are other things we can do.

For instance, if we use **asynchronous** communication as a primary means of class communication, we have a wealth of student writing data to investigate. We could look at things ranging from level of engagement to conversational posting habits, from error trends to the level of introspection in student posts. We could use students' commentary about their own writing and thinking processes in portfolio-type artifacts that demonstrate the kind of communication engagement that occurred in the class. We could also use the e-environment to investigate student course habits and how they relate to student success. I investigated student posting habits briefly in a post on my weblog, and then delved more thoroughly into this topic for an article. I found a noticeable final grade difference between those who posted early on message board **threads** and those who delayed. The early posters did better in the course (Warnock, "Early").

Do students who follow up their posts have a different experience? Does post length have any meaning in terms of course outcome? How about number of errors? We could perform a number of interesting, localized assessments of our own class practices using the student texts generated and then archived right in our own courses. Because of the large amount of informal writing we can easily assign and use online, can we find quantitative or qualitative differences in the writing that students do in this environment? How do students collaborate online, in peer review and team-based projects? What works in e-collaborations? What doesn't? Rather than simply ask students how much they liked a course, can we tap into ways of measuring their engagement through their written work?

We also can consider our efforts in terms of doing no harm—bolstering the no significant difference aspect of online instruction by thinking about retention, student evaluations, and perhaps even student grades in future writing courses. Hundreds of studies have shown that there is no difference in teaching modalities, so we might not want to spend time reproducing older work, but we can view our work as writing teachers as opening new opportunities for broader assessments. What we would be doing is rethinking assessments of online learning in general and applying them specifically to the **OWcourse**.

There is another built-in advantage to using technological learning tools, specifically the **CMS**: these tools have tremendous capabilities for keeping a record of student behavior. I know this can get kind of creepy, and I always frame my efforts to delve into such records constructively, but the tools exist in most any CMS to see the number of times our students have posted, the number of times they have viewed material on the CMS, and even the amount of time they have spent on the course website. Using these tools, we can actually quantify some student behaviors.

Increasingly, it's an assessment-based education world. In order to support our work, like any other group of teachers, writing instructors should be seeking ways, in our own classes, program-wide, and across the field, to demonstrate the strengths and weaknesses of what we are doing. A variety of resources can help develop the framework of such studies, including the impressive anthology *Digital Writing Research* by Heidi McKee and Dànielle DeVoss. As of 2008, a CCCC group, chaired by Beth Hewett, has been looking into best practices in online writing instruction. Check out the CompPile website for a search on *assessment*. Or delve into assessment resources and model articles on sites like MERLOT or Sloan-C, or in one of the many journals dedicated to online learning, such as the *Online Journal of Distance Learning Administration*. Much of the research focus in online learning has been on so-called "content" courses. I believe there is an open vista before us for assessment of writing-centered courses in this environment. Exploring it will help us continue to validate our teaching work to external audiences, our students, and, of course, ourselves.

Pre-term Questions

- ◆ *What might indicate that your students are learning effectively in your online classes?* Think about the same kind of question for your onsite courses.

- ◆ *What classroom measures could you use to reflect on your teaching?* Could you measure student responses, your own interaction, the way students dialogue with each other? If you are a first-term teacher, you probably have enough on your mind, but these measures could help you begin to frame an assessment mindset toward your own courses.

CHAPTER EIGHTEEN

Resources: A World of Help Out There

Online writing teachers might not be aware of the many good resources available. This chapter looks at some of them.

Y ou'll find numerous citations throughout this book that support the ideas I have presented and the specific pedagogical approaches I have discussed. Here, in annotated bibliographic form, I describe some valuable resources that you might use when preparing to teach an **OWcourse**. The list is organized by category, so some sources are listed more than once. My hope is that this bibliography will be helpful if you are looking for a few resources about a specific area of online teaching. I don't pretend that this is an exhaustive list.

General Online/Distance Teaching Resources

There are many resources for teaching online; as I mentioned in the Introduction, the gap in training materials is not in content-based courses, but in specific strategies for OWcourses. The MERLOT website has hundreds of **learning object**s and websites about language that are open source so faculty may use them as they see fit. According to the MERLOT site, much of this material is peer reviewed. The Sloan-C website states, "The Sloan Consortium is an institutional and professional leadership organization dedicated to integrating online education into the mainstream of higher education, helping institutions and individual educators improve the quality, scale, and breadth of online education"

(Sloan-C, par. 1). This is another site full of teaching and learning materials for those working in the online learning environment.

Conrad and Donaldson's *Engaging the Online Learner* provides clear instructions about creating activities for online learning situations and provides many examples of how those activities might look. The authors also included a chapter on using games and simulations. Ko and Rossen's *Teaching Online*; Levine's *Making Distance Education Work*; Smith's *Conquering the Content*; Dawley's *The Tools for Successful Online Teaching*; and Hanna, Glowacki-Dudki, and Conceicao-Runlee's *147 Practical Tips for Teaching Online Groups* all provide practical advice for teaching online. Ken White and Bob Weight's *The Online Teaching Guide* is a "survival manual" for teaching online (vi). Rena Palloff and Keith Pratt have published a series of books about working with online learners, including *The Virtual Student*.

Susanmarie Harrington, Rebecca Rickly, and Michael Day's *The Online Writing Classroom* is one of the few books that specifically addresses the concerns of those who teach *writing* online. It contains a good mix of practical advice with theoretical background about what online writing teachers are trying to accomplish. Hewett and Ehmann's *Preparing Educators for Online Writing Instruction* lays a solid computers and composition foundation in describing one-on-one tutoring and mentoring in the online environment; this book's compositional work strongly informed my own book.

Collaboration

Many books about online learning mention how group activities might work in this environment. For instance, Bender spent a chapter on group activities in her *Discussion-based Online Teaching to Enhance Student Learning*. A somewhat dense text that draws from different methodologies but is nevertheless useful for thinking about collaboration, is Valerie Sessa and Manuel London's *Work Group Learning*. Barber's essay, "Effective Teaching in the Online Classroom: Thoughts and Recommendations," in Harrington, Rickly, and Day's *The Online Writing Classroom*, advised teachers not to abandon collaborative projects in the online course and described how technology can aid such projects. Palloff and Pratt also investigated working with online learners in collaborative settings in *Collaborating Online*.

Computers and Composition

The theory behind this book is driven by the work of many computers and composition scholars, and much recent work in that area finds its way directly into the preceding chapters. If you are interested in some of the earlier foundational computers and composition work, here is a brief—and perhaps quirky in what it includes and what it leaves out—list of some significant materials: Bolter's *Writing Space*, Hawisher and Selfe's *Evolving Perspectives on Computers and Composition Studies*, Landow's *Hypertext*, Lanham's *The Electronic Word*, Selfe and Hilligoss's *Literacy and Computers*, Hawisher and LeBlanc's *Re-Imagining Computers and Composition*, Haas's *Writing Technology*, Hawisher and Selfe's *Passions, Pedagogies, and 21st Century Technologies*, Taylor and Ward's *Literacy Theory in the Age of the Internet*, and Selfe's *Technology and Literacy in the Twenty-First Century*.

Content Delivery

Because most online courses have been content based, almost any online teaching resource will offer content development suggestions. *Conquering the Content* is a great book to help you set up the initial content in your course, and Smith included helpful material about thinking your way through the development of your first online course. She described in depth how to chunk course material based on brain-processing concepts and included detailed forms in the appendixes to stimulate your thinking about preparing and organizing your online course. Wolf's website, "Efficient and Effective Organization of an Online Class," provides a succinct Web guide to help you stay organized while teaching online. Marilyn Fullmer-Umari's chapter "Getting Ready:

The Syllabus and Other Online Indispensables," in White and Weight's *The Online Teaching Guide,* offers helpful instruction about delivering lectures online and focuses on adapting your communication styles and materials.

Copyright

If you want to further educate yourself about electronic copyright, see Renee Hobbs, Peter Jaszi, and Pat Aufderheide's *The Cost of Copyright Confusion for Media Literacy* or Martine Courant Rife's *The Importance of Understanding and Utilizing Fair Use in Educational Contexts.*

Effectiveness of Online and Hybrid Learning

If you are asked to provide proof of the effectiveness of online learning, the Western Cooperative for Educational Telecommunications's *No Significant Difference Phenomenon* website is your ticket. This site, a companion to Thomas L. Russell's book, *The No Significant Difference Phenomenon,* provides more than 300 studies that show that e-learning is equivalent to onsite learning. In numerous e-forums and **listservs**, I have seen experienced online teachers become frustrated as people replicate the many studies that show no significant difference in learning efficacy; to them, it's time to move on. In the *Chronicle of Higher Education,* Jeffrey Young's short piece, "Study Finds **Hybrid** Courses Just as Effective as Traditional Ones," noted that students in hybrid health courses appear to learn as effectively as in onsite courses (par. 1).

Hybrid Courses

In *Blended Learning in Higher Education,* Garrison and Vaughan stated, "Blended learning is the thoughtful fusion of face-to-face and online learning experiences" (5). Their book provides thorough guidance on creating hybrids, including course design advice for specific courses and focused strategies. In *Teaching Online*, Ko and Rossen offered many good examples of how instructors have converted courses into hybrid formats, including a list of questions to help you with such a conversion. Throughout her *Discussion-Based Online Teaching to Enhance Student Learning*, Bender mentioned hybrids and noted that through them, "different learning styles and methods can be accommodated" (xvii). Another resource in this area is Kaye Thorne's *Blended Learning: How to Integrate Online and Traditional Learning*.

CMS Comparisons

As I mentioned in Chapter 3, Mount Holyoke College, EduTools, and Maricopa Community Colleges have sites that allow you to compare the strengths and weaknesses of different **CMS** packages. In her book *The Tools for Successful Online Teaching*, Dawley looked quickly at various kinds of CMS.

Message Boards and Asynchronous Discussions

Collison and his coauthors' *Facilitating Online Learning* is an excellent resource; it describes how teachers can moderate online conversations and includes a lengthy account of the different roles that online moderators can assume. Salmon's oft-cited *E-Moderating* provides great detail to help teachers get better at e-moderating, "a new way of teaching" (7) in the twenty-first century, with solid insight and examples of moderating students' electronic writing. Bender's *Discussion-based Online Teaching to Enhance Student Learning* focuses on text-based, **asynchronous** online teaching. In her chapter in *The Online Teaching Guide*, "Online Facilitation: Individual and Group Possibilities," Addesso anchored her comments in the idea that facilitating e-discussion is in many ways similar to facilitating onsite class discussions.

Peer Review

Many online teaching guides provide light coverage of peer review. However, Breuch's *Virtual Peer Review* is a focused book about the topic of peer review with technology tools. Breuch has supported her conversation about peer review in online settings with theory, while offering practical guidelines on implementing peer review (132–33).

Syllabus Creation

Ko and Rossen's *Teaching Online* includes a detailed chapter about creating an online syllabus. Of course, Wilbert McKeachie's classic *McKeachie's Teaching Tips* is helpful for general syllabus creation.

Synchronous Course Communication

Ko and Rossen's *Teaching Online* offers a lengthy checklist of suggestions for running an effective chat. In *Making Distance Education Work*, Levine peppered his conversation with references to **synchronous** modalities. And although often focusing on computer-mediated communication in general, Pamela Gay's article "Improving Classroom Culture" discussed ways of using good pedagogy in synchronous communications.

In an older but still useful article about teaching with audio and video, Michael Miller and Dann Husmann identified specific strategies to help instructors prepare to teach using two-way audio and one-way video technology.

New resources are constantly being developed for online instruction. In this necessarily incomplete chapter, I have offered a range of materials that have influenced my thinking on these topics. You will no doubt expand upon this list.

Pre-term Questions

♦ *Which areas will you most need to address?* Pick a few resources, commit yourself to acquiring them, and begin reading about those areas.

♦ *How will you organize the various electronic resources that are available?*

Teaching Writing with Technology: A Personality-Driven Endeavor

I will conclude by discussing the idea that teaching is ultimately a personality-driven endeavor and that the tools of online teaching can allow you to extend your personality in ways that may surprise even the most resistant technophobes.

This book has focused on ways of maximizing the use of learning technologies to teach writing. Many layers of interface lie between our students and the knowledge they seek, regardless of the medium of instruction: desks, term bills, advisors, books, *us*. Students must learn how to work with and through these interfaces to maximize their experience in our classes and to improve their writing. In online learning, as Hanna, Glowacki-Dudki, and Conceicao-Runlee said, the technology is "always present" and demands attention from teachers and their students (xviii). However, in the context of the OWcourse, I believe that the growing use of technological tools can lessen the educational interface, because what we are asking many of our screenage students to do in OWcourses is actually closer to their "normal" writing practices than ever before.

Think about it. Arguments rage about the quality of the e-writing our students regularly engage in during their online experiences on social networking sites like Facebook or MySpace, with text messaging, or in the blogosphere; yet to me it's plain that no matter how we define it, they write a lot more than my generation did. They are writing all the time, almost frantically using textual language to communicate with one another, and coming up with remarkably clever ways to communicate their message to the intended receiver (just ask any parents who can't decipher their children's text messages). In the *Washington Post*, Howard Gardner wrote, "Literacy—or an ensemble of literacies—will continue to thrive, but in forms and formats we can't yet envision" (B1). We, as writing teachers, are highly empowered in this environment to help channel the natural writing that students are doing anyway into a class experience. I'm reminded of a recent listserv conversation I followed, which discussed ways to use a 140-*character* writing assignment, based, of course, on text-messaging practices.

This leads me to what I consider one of the most basic premises of writing instruction: teaching is a personality-driven endeavor, an *art*, especially the teaching of writing. There is no easy formula to describe the kind of personality that is best for teaching, but it's increasingly clear to me that the way you interface with your students helps determine what they will get out of your writing classes. You may accept this idea, but the next idea may have surprised some of you before you read this book: the tools that can assist you in teaching writing online can extend and reshape your teaching personality—often in productive ways. In *Discussion-Based Online Teaching to Enhance Student Learning*, Bender's focus was on the "*human* implications of teaching and learning by communicating through the Internet" (xv). The technology can be cool, but how you and your students use technology to work with course, teaching, and learning goals will ultimately determine the success of OWcourses.

Your Online Persona

I began this book by noting that one of the key factors you should consider as you embark on teaching online is *who* you are as a teacher. You must consider this carefully, just as you would in an onsite class. Again, the tools of teaching online can seem to create a barrier between you and your students, but they can also allow you to expand and shape this personality in highly productive, imaginative ways. Although you could argue that we each create a personality "shell" as a teacher, regardless of the teaching medium, you can customize this shell in fascinating ways in an online classroom. In *Literacy and Computers*, Cynthia Selfe and Susan Hilligoss emphasized what became a framework for computers and composition work: we should ask ourselves what model of literacy will guide our discussion of technology (79). If we place technology first, we may be making a mistake, as I have argued throughout this book.

Think about how people use technology as a tool to develop personality in various forms in online worlds. The online, text-based interactive experience of the older environments like MOOs and MUDs, which Dibbell described spectacularly in *My Tiny Life*, has been updated by communities like Second Life, where people can shift core aspects of themselves, including gender and even species, to create visual avatars that interact with others.

In the online writing class, you can use your words to craft the kind of personality you think is appropriate to help your students learn. Chad Lewis suggested ways to "improve online warmth," including describing your personal setting while writing, offering jokes, or personalizing your text. He even suggested using emoticons (18). As I mentioned when discussing assignments, I sometimes use an interlocutor who is always the devil's advocate to coax argument out of students. Because this interlocutor is not really me, I am not personally attached to the argument, as we teachers might tend to be with our stances. Students can wage arguments with this persona without feeling that they are battling the almighty, all-knowing and, most important, all-grading teacher.

But forget slick alter egos. Your standard online self in the writing class can be someone who is perpetually helpful and supportive, always upbeat in the face of deadlines and student questions. It might even be easier to sustain this kind of personality in the online environment than it is onsite. Especially if you use asynchronous communications, you can really put on your game face when you teach online—so you're always "on," to your students' benefit.

Since the beginning of online instructional modes, people have discussed one of the advantages of "talking" via text: you have the chance to more freely be yourself. (Recall the classic 1993 *New Yorker* cartoon, in which a dog at a computer monitor says to another dog, "On the Internet, nobody knows you're a dog.") Hawisher noted this early, in terms of instruction, pointing out the potential democraticizing that could take place in the Internet-facilitated class (88). You can use these tools to be more available, more receptive to student ideas, and perhaps friendlier than you are in an onsite class. For instance, consider an icebreaker class in which students interview each other and then relate details about one another to the rest of the class. This can be a challenging class for a teacher to run. Teachers are supposed to, in impromptu fashion, respond to the likes, dislikes, and personality traits of a room full of people they have just met! Online, you can have a similar icebreaker, but you can interject in a more measured way because you have time to think and then write responses to students. At the conclusion of the online icebreaker, you can respond as a friendly, concerned, interested person to every single student in your class.

Teaching and Personality

In closing, I want to return to the beginning of this book. A teacher's personality is important to teaching success, and Janet Johnson and Karen Card found that does not change online, as teacher—and peer—immediacy and "social presence" are key factors in student achievement (15). I think the teaching of writing is even more personality-driven. All the tools and support in the world will not help me teach writing to a group of students who feel alienated or perhaps even disrespectful of me. I could be supplied with the finest syllabus and support and still come up short. But you, with a poorly designed core syllabus and little institutional support, could wow and amaze your students, helping them become better writers.

This is not a plea to be chummy with students. In fact, in my experience, chumminess can be the kiss of death. There is no clear model for what breeds successful teacher personalities, nor is it fully clear if personality is even a cause or an effect of student learning (Henderson and Nash 205). But whatever the strange mix of traits, one thing is clear: you should consider how your personality influences the way you interact with your students.

What will they need? How will they respond to that key inter-action, your commentary about their written texts? As Ko and Rossen said, "The fact that someone has word-processed all of his or her lectures and transferred graphics to HTML pages doesn't mean that a course has been converted. In fact, this isn't even the first step!" (45). In a similar vein, Levine said that the "delivery of information" view of learning is like a "supermarket approach to instruction": "stock the shelves" with the content and "wait for the customers." Instead, he advocates the "relationship view of teaching and learning" ("Creating" 18). Migrating your material online shouldn't mean that you flatten the teaching personality you have worked on for years. Instead, it should mean that you find new ways to express yourself, which is precisely what we ask students to do in written environments.

Students need to "see" you—and each other—in a certain way to have a productive class experience. Research is ongoing about what that way might look like, and it is beyond question that different students need different things. What I want to leave you with is the idea that teaching, for better or worse, is a function of personality, and the technological tools at our disposal can make a difference in helping us sharpen and direct that personality in ways that help us to be better teachers of writing.

APPENDIXES: TEACHING MATERIALS

Appendix A: Sample Syllabus

My syllabus from Persuasive Writing & Reading, Winter 2008.

Drexel University Department of English & Philosophy Winter 2008
English 102 (sect. 900) Online: Persuasive Writing and Reading

Instructor: Dr. Scott Warnock
Office location: MacAlister 5043
Office hours: MW 10:00 to 11:30

Course Bb Vista site: learning.dcollege.net
Phone: 215-895-0377 or 856-829-0626
Email: sjwarnock@drexel.edu

REQUIRED TEXTS

Wood, Nancy. *Perspectives on Argument.* 5th ed. Upper Saddle River: Pearson Prentice Hall, 2007.

Kirszner, Laurie and Stephen Mandell. *The Brief Handbook.* 5th ed. Boston: Thomson, 2007.

COURSE GOALS AND LEARNING OUTCOMES

The Freshman Writing Program at Drexel is a three-course, year-long sequence that has a specific focus each term. During the year, among other things, you will learn to

1. Appreciate and respond to diverse audiences
2. Use writing and reading for inquiry, learning, thinking, and communicating
3. Understand writing as a process
4. Use research to develop, support, and enhance your ideas

English 102 builds on the concepts presented in English 101: You will continue to develop critical thinking skills, using materials from reading and research to support your ideas. The purpose of English 102 is to help you learn how to develop clear, convincing arguments. In English 102, you will learn to construct arguments in defense of a thesis, idea, or claim that requires support from sources found through research or from selected assigned readings. In the process, you will learn to evaluate sources, to consider and refute opposing arguments, and to document various forms of evidence. You will also develop an understanding of how the ability to construct effective arguments enables you to take part more fully in the public and professional debates that affect you and the lives of others.

To achieve the goals of English 102, you will learn how to:
- Read actively and critically
- Reflect upon a topic, specifically how to assess audience and establish purpose and how to use a variety of invention strategies productively
- Research a topic, specifically how to access, evaluate, paraphrase, and use information from a variety of sources, and cite your sources accurately, using a recognized and accepted system such as MLA format
- Revise for content, structure, and cohesion
- Edit writing to ensure correct grammar, sentence structure, spelling, diction, punctuation, and mechanics
- Construct and evaluate effective arguments, using a variety of rhetorical strategies
- Prepare and participate in a team project

COURSE REQUIREMENTS/GRADING (1000 points)

Project 1: Letter to the editor	100 points
Project 2: Taking a position	150 points
Project 3: Persuasion	150 points
Team project	100 points
Informal writing/ELC work	450 points
Quizzes	50 points
Participation	+/- 10 to 20 points

Projects
I will provide you with detailed information about each of the major projects as they are assigned, starting in week one with Project 1. Note that you have a substantial *team project* in this course.

Informal writing/Electronic Learning Community (ELC) Work
Each week, you will have a number of assignments I am calling ELC requirements. Many of those ELC requirements will take place on the Discussions on our course Bb Vista site. Your schedule will be provided to you each week via a Weekly Plan, which will describe what is due and when. If you are new to Bb Vista, please take a quick tutorial under Student Resources on your My Course List page.

Quizzes

We will have a brief quiz on most of the readings. The bottom line is the quizzes are designed to help you (and your grade): if you do the readings, you can expect to do well on the quizzes. Quiz rules:

- All quizzes are timed. You will only have a few minutes to complete each quiz, but, if you read, I assure you that you'll find the quizzes quite manageable (and, I daresay, even easy).
- The quizzes will be offered for a set period of time, and then they will no longer be available. There are no make-ups for a missed quiz.
- The quizzes are all short answer.
- You may drop one quiz (actually, I will do this for you).

COURSE POLICIES

Academic honesty

All students must abide by Drexel University's academic honesty policies. If an act of academic dishonesty is determined to have occurred, for a first offense, one of the following sanctions will be imposed, depending on the severity of the offense: 1) 0% for the assignment; 2) failure for entire course without the possibility to withdraw; this information, based on the decision of the faculty member and the department head shall be reported to the Office of Judicial Affairs. The incident will result in an official disciplinary record for the student(s).

Note that plagiarism is not limited to copying a passage from a source word for word. If you acquire specific information from a source, you must acknowledge that source, even if you have used your own words and paraphrased that information. Review *The Brief Wadsworth Handbook* Parts 3 and 4 for acceptable ways of acknowledging the work of other writers.

Any academic honesty infraction beyond a first offense is subject to the sanctions described above, as well as to disciplinary sanctions that may be imposed through the University judicial process, administered through the Division for Student Life and Administrative Services/Office of Judicial Affairs. These sanctions may include suspension or expulsion from the University (Drexel University Student Handbook, 2005-2006 ed. [http://www.drexel.edu/studentlife/images/0506Handbook.pdf]).

Accountability

I am here to work with you and help you, but you are accountable for your performance in the course. If you miss class, hand in work late, or are otherwise negligent in your duties as a student, I ask that you take responsibility for your actions. Your accountability starts with your careful reading of this syllabus. As part of your responsibilities, you must make it a habit to check the **course homepage** regularly. Set yourself a schedule to check it.

Disability
Students with disabilities who request accommodations and services at Drexel need to present a current accommodation verification letter (AVL) to faculty before accommodations can be made. AVLs are issued by the Office of Disability Services (ODS). For additional information, contact the ODS at www.drexel.edu/edt/disability, 3201 Arch St., Ste. 210, Philadelphia, PA 19104, V 215-895-1401 or TTY 215-895-2299.

Drop/withdraw
Students have until the end of the 2nd week of the term to drop a course without financial responsibility. Undergraduates have until the end of the 6th week of the term to withdraw with financial responsibility, according to the University's sliding scale. See http://www.drexel.edu/bursar/tuition_credits.asp for details on the sliding scale.

File-naming conventions
To help organize the work in the course, please adhere to the following conventions when naming assignment files. Name the file with your first name, last initial, assignment name, and then a one-word description of the assignment. So my first draft of project one would look like this: ScottWproj1draftfear.doc.

Late assignments
The learning in this course requires in-depth reading, reflection, writing, discussion, independent work, and team work. To achieve our goals, you must complete your work in a timely manner. Late projects and assignments will be penalized.

Library skills
You must know how to use the library resources. Be sure to go to the library's New Students' Guide to the Libraries: http://www.library.drexel.edu/about/studentguide.html. All 102 classes have a library visit planned at some point in the term.

Technology
Obviously, you need easy access to Bb Vista to participate in this class. You must also have access to some type of media software such as RealPlayer. If you have trouble accessing Bb Vista because of your particular computer setup, you're going to find this course difficult; you will be unhappy. Important: Ask yourself this question: "What will happen to my participation in this course if my computer goes

down?" If the answer is "I am doomed," then you should withdraw and register for a face-to-face section of 101. <u>You need to have backup technology plans, because a down computer will not excuse you from the work in the course.</u>

You must also have an active <u>Drexel</u> email account (it is easy to set up your Drexel account to forward mail to another account).

Turnitin.com
I will ask you to turn in your major written assignments to Turnitin.com. The Turnitin.com drop box for your assignments will be located on our Bb Vista site.

DREXEL UNIVERSITY WRITING CENTER

The Writing Center is located in 0032 MacAlister (x6633). Qualified tutors will help you work through any writing assignment you are having trouble completing successfully. Call or visit the Writing Center and make an appointment for a conference with a tutor—you don't even need to bring a paper with you.

You may be particularly interested in the Center's electronic tutoring services, E-Writer. You can submit a draft, some ideas, or some questions. The Writing Center's Webpage has more details: www.drexel.edu/writingcenter. Stop by the Center; you may find it's one of the best places on campus to help you enhance your writing (and thinking).

MAJOR DUE DATES

This should give you a general idea of when projects are due, but the schedule and assignments are subject to change.

Week 3	Project #1 final draft
Week 6	Project #2 final draft
Week 9	Project #3 final draft
Week 10	Team Website

Participating in an Online Writing Course
For some of you, this will be your first experience in an online course. You'll no doubt find this to be a different experience than that of a face-to-face (f2f) class. Following are some things to think about as you begin this online learning experience. I also have prepared a more extensive list of frequently asked questions about online writing courses here: http://www.drexel.edu/coas/engphil/online.asp.

Follow the Weekly Plans
I create careful Weekly Plans each week to help you stay organized. If you closely read and follow the Weekly Plans, you significantly increase your chances of success in here.

Deadlines

It is crucial that you adhere closely to the class deadlines. In fact, you should ask yourself a question: "Am I self-motivated enough to meet these deadlines?" If the answer is "no," then you should probably switch to a f2f section of English 102. I have seen too many students stubbornly resist the obvious: they are not good candidates for an online class because they couldn't meet the deadlines on their own. Unfortunately, many of those students have had poor outcomes in the course as a result.

Contact

Most of our communications will take place via:

<u>Discussions</u>

Bb Vista Discussions will make up the major part of our interaction this quarter, as you can see from the course requirements.

<u>Email</u>

You need to become familiar with your Drexel email account. That account can easily be forwarded to another account, but I will use your Drexel account to send you mail. We'll do a lot of corresponding that way. Do NOT use Bb Vista email.

<u>Chat</u>

Sometimes we will correspond via chat, particularly the day before a paper is due. Chats will be voluntary.

I will spend time checking email and Discussions for course messages each weekday morning (around 9:00 Eastern Standard Time [EST]) and in the afternoon (around 4:00 EST). The day before major assignments are due, I will be available at other times. If there is ever an emergency, please do not hesitate to call me.

There is a temptation in an online course for you to think of your professor as a robot who never sleeps. While you are college students, and you may do some of your most productive work at 2 in the morning, I am an old(ish) man who goes to bed at 10:30. Remember that when you email me in the wee hours of the night and can't understand why I haven't responded to you.

You can also reach me by phone at the numbers listed on the Syllabus. The home office is just that, a home office, meaning that I work there and expect work-related phone calls. Don't be shy about calling that number if you need me.

The three-dimensional me can be found in MacAlister 5043. My office hours are Monday and Wednesday from 10:00 to 11:30, but I am around a lot more than that and will make every effort to be available if you need to see me in person.

Space
You're working online. Where should you do this work? You need to treat the time you are writing and thinking about the class material as real class time, and therefore you need a quiet place to do that. In fact, you will have a lot more success in college if you learn to carve out a quiet space when you study. Ask your friends, roommates, and/or family to give you a break during a set time each day, or you'll need to find a good, quiet place on campus or somewhere else where you can study. I know you are probably all skilled multitaskers, but if you get into bad study habits as a freshman, they will be hard to break later.

Feeling isolated?
Remember, while our class is online, I'm a real, live human being who has an office on campus. If you have concerns, feel free to stop in and talk to me during my office hours or at least call me.

As we progress, you may not like what's happening in this online course. If you truly feel that this experience is not for you, you can switch to a f2f section early in the quarter.

Appendix B: Sample Weekly Plan
Week 2: January 11 to January 17

Again, please simply follow the directions in order, from top to bottom.

This week, the focus is on topics for Project 1 and doing some more reading and writing to get acclimated to the course ideas.

You'll note that if you wait too long on the readings and discussions that you could have a lot of work to do on Tuesday and Wednesday.

What do I do?	What are the specific instructions? Where do I find the work or the assignment?	When is it due? (All times EST)
READ	Read the following: • *Allyn & Bacon:* Chap. 9, "Writing an Informative Essay or Report" and end-of-chapter readings 208-38; • *BbV* (in Course Materials folder): Spinnuzi, "Guest Editor's Introduction: Technical Communication in the Age of Distributed Work" 265-77.	You'll want to have read by **Wednesday**, January 14 so you can complete the quiz and work on the Discussion topics.
TAKE a QUIZ	Quiz 2 can be found in the Quizzes folder on the course Homepage. Again, remember that for the quizzes: 1. I am looking for VERY short answers. 2. The quiz answers can be informal. I don't grade them on spelling, etc. 3. I am not looking to trick you. If you've read, you should be able to complete the quiz successfully in a few minutes with no problem.	The quiz will be available **Wednesday** from 9:30 am to midnight. You will have <u>5 minutes</u> to complete it. If you miss the quiz, there are no make-ups. I will drop one quiz though.
WRITE and READ	You did a solid job in week 1, but you might want to review the Discussion guidelines on the syllabus before you start on this week's HLC work: • **Project 1 topic Discussion:** Follow the instructions on the Discussion thread "Project 1 topics." You will be asked to propose a topic as **ONE** primary post, and then you will write **ONE** secondary post in response to one of your colleague's topics. • **Reading Discussions:** You will have several reading Discussion options this week. You will post **TWO** primary and **ONE** secondary post on our reading Discussions. Don't forget to stay current on the Discussions, and make sure you *read* through everything on the message boards.	Post your primary post by **Wednesday** night. (I know some of you are night owls, and while I don't want to encourage procrastination, you can post as late as you like on Wednesday night/Thursday wee morning.) Post your secondary posts by **Friday**, January 16, at 4:00 pm. **This is a hard deadline.** Complete all your posts for the "Project 1 topics" thread by **Thursday** evening.
MODERATE (one of you)	This week our moderator will be David __. I will be in touch with him, and then he will serve as moderator for some of our Discussions this week. He will be an active voice in encouraging conversation, and he will provide a summary at the end of the week. Thanks to David for going first here.	--

Appendix C: A Sample Message Board Conversation

Below I provide an extended abstract of part of a conversation that took place in a composition course I taught in 2005. While this is certainly a strong conversation, I chose it because I think it is emblematic of the types of conversations that occur in this environment; in other words, I am not simply showing you an unreasonable example of what you might expect from students in this environment. This is an extended example, so you may not need to read everything, but I think that it helps demonstrate what students might accomplish in this environment.

In addition to the actual posts, I have provided a few brief annotations and some highlight to indicate key areas of interest.

Subject: That well-traveled road

Message no. 641
Author: Scott Warnock
Date: Monday, April 25, 2005 10:06am

Hi all,
Frost's "The Road Not Taken" is one of his most famous poems. It alternately maddens and delights, for some see it as a simple statement that is overanalyzed while others see it as a poem of vast complexity (perhaps much like "Stopping by Woods...").

I use a straight-forward prompt to start things off.

Why does Frost focus on the road NOT taken? What difference is there between the two paths? What is significant about his choice—and his prediction of his reflections about that choice?
You too have made this choice,
Prof. Warnock

Subject: re: That well-traveled road

Message no. 648 [Reply of: no. 641]
Author: Rene
Date: Monday, April 25, 2005 12:37pm

I think that a person's outlook on the future, and maybe even parts of their past help shape how they interpret this poem. This poem is very powerful and can have many different meanings to different people. To me, I was most able to relate with the disappointment Frost felt in not being able to explore every path in life. "And sorry I could not travel both"

The first student replies directly to the prompt.

(line 2). **Frost knows that if he chooses this path, he will have little opportunity in life to go back and take the other path.** "I doubted if I should ever come back" (line 15). Each path leads to an unknown; one never knows how their life is going to turn out. People are faced with decisions every day. Very seldom does the person know the true consequences of the decisions he or she is about to make. For me, I often play the game, "What if..." "What if, I didn't go to Drexel...?" "What if I wasn't into sports in high school, what else would I have done with my time?" I think this poem represents the what ifs of the world. What if he had taken the other path? He will never know, because he made a decision and stuck to it. The other main part of this poem that I can relate to is he took the path that was "less traveled by" (line 19). For some reason he was obliged to take the path that had obviously been less traveled by. He went against the grain of society. He made his own decision, and stuck to it. The great part about the end is, although he still has regrets that he will never be able to experience both paths, he is very proud of the decision he did make. He took the path that was obviously less traveled on, "And that made all the difference" (line 20).

One part that I really liked was, "And both the morning equally lay In leaves no step had trodden black" (Lines 11-12). **It took me awhile to grasp what I thought Frost meant by these two lines. Finally, I came up with the paths were covered with leaves, there were no footprints, it was like new. I guess every person comes to a point in their life where they have to make a decision that undoubtedly, many other people had to make. However, the predicament and decision is still new to this person. Obviously, other people came to this point and had to make a decision about which path to take, however, the leaves covered up their markings, making it like a "new path" for Frost. Any other ideas as to what these two lines mean?**

> The student draws on direct evidence in the reply.

Subject: re: That well-traveled road

Message no. 653 [Reply of: no. 648]
Author: Brad
Date: Monday, April 25, 2005 4:33pm

Rene,
I agree with you. The narrator is stuck with a difficult decision, and he isn't sure which path to take. Both

seem about equally promising to him, though one was less travelled.

> The next post replies to a colleague, not me. He also closes with a question.

I think when it says "And both that morning equally lay In leaves no step had trodden black" (lines 11-12) it is talking about the decision having yet to be made, even after sleeping on it. Both paths seemed to be about equal (both that morning equally lay). And, he hadn't yet committed to either path (In leaves no step had trodden black). The next line reinforces this, as he "kept the first for another day." It seems as though the individual in the poem is struggling if he should even make a choice at all - "I doubted if I should ever come back" (line 15).

I think the decision was definately new to him, but I don't think other people could have experienced quite the same choice.

What I want to know is, when he .. "took the one less traveled by," (line 19) was that a positive difference? Because he feels like he "shall be telling this with a sigh somewhere ages and ages hence" (line 16-17). Any ideas?

Subject: re: That well-traveled road
Message no. 689 [Reply of: no. 648]
Author: Scott Warnock
Date: Wednesday, April 27, 2005 3:40pm

Hi Rene,
For some reason, the line "I doubted if I should ever come back" (line 15) actually chokes me up. I agree with you.
Prof. W.

> I nudge the conversation as a "reflective guide."

Subject: re: That well-traveled road
Message no. 651 [Reply of: no. 641]
Author: Shaona
Date: Monday, April 25, 2005 4:15pm

The overanalysis of this poem infuriates me too, but I am also guilty of trying to make it have an ultimate meaning. The reason I think this poem is that famous is that it is versatile enough to be interpreted personally, as you said, we have all made this choice.

> The next post couches frustration intelligently.

Frost may have concentrated on the road less traveled, even though he wishes to travel both, simply out
of primitive human curiousity. Chances are, he may have
guessed that physically the well-traveled path would
lead to another town or landscape with opportunities,
but the unstoppable demon of curiousity that's a part of
most humans made him take and wonder about the road less
traveled by.

Frost finishes this poem in an interesting manner. "Two
roads diverged in a wood, and I--I took the one less
traveled by, And that has made all the difference." (880)
He does not say whether it was a positive or negative
difference, perhaps simply implying it was greatly different from the original path he was tak-
ing. Many people refer to those lines
when they want to aspire to something
they are not certain they are capable
of, my mother often refers to that line
in a positive manner. I think Frost
kept it ambiguous to leave it open to
interpretation.

> The writer
> cleverly
> synthesizes
> her thinking
> here.

**Ultimately, a well traveled road and a road not taken
are paths that simply consist of different scenery. They
may lead to different locations or the same location,
it's the experience of traveling down that road that
creates character.** There is no right or wrong, there is
simply a choice of atmosphere, the end is never discussed in this poem and the goal of his journey is not
brought into context. It could have been the yellow
wood of his soul or just a yellow wood in New England.
That is the beauty of decisions, he shows, that they
come in all forms, symbolically or literally, spiritu-
ally or logically, and that the Journey that they create
for the decision maker makes "all the difference"

Subject: re: That well-traveled road
Message no. 773 [Reply of: no. 651]
Author: Janet
Date: Saturday, April 30, 2005 8:26pm

**Shaona, you know as strange as this
may sound, I never just looked at this
poem and just thought about paths in
the road. I always just figured it was
supposed to be symbolic, so I never
pictured literal paths in the woods. I
like thinking about it this way.**

> Another direct
> response to a
> colleague—and
> a closing sup-
> port comment.

You make a very good point about whether or not the difference is positive or negative. I had just assumed it was positive because that is the way people who quote the line portray it. It never even crossed my mind that it might not be. When I think about it, different seems a little negative to me. Like when you try on an outfit and you ask someone how it looks. If they say it looks different, the immediate thought is that it looks bad and to go change. Of course different can be a good thing, it just depends on your interpretation of change. I think that this poem is just simply saying the choices you make today affect your future. It can be over analyzed and ripped apart, but in the end that seems like the general message.

Good Job!

Subject: re: That well-traveled road
Message no. 666 [Reply of: no. 641]
Author: Julie
Date: Tuesday, April 26, 2005 12:42pm

I usually like poems about love and all that romantic stuff, but for some reason this poem really strikes me as a good one! Good pick Professor!

A brief context comment. She then talks directly to me below.

Frost focuses on "the road not taken" because as people, it is our nature to go along with the crowd. It's easier to follow someone else's steps because you know what to expect. This "road" is the usually the first option that comes to mind because it is sometimes scary to make your own path. He was even considering walking down the easy way, "And looked down one as far as I could." (880)

The difference between the two paths is that one is rather worn-down, clearer and easier to go through. The other is not as worn-down but just as interesting to walk through, "Because it was grassy and wanted wear..." (880) The significance of his choice is that he was willing to divert from the ordinary and make a path of his own, even if it's not the most popular or the easiest. He took a different way and was happier because he did, "I took the one less traveled by, And that has made all the difference." (880) You are right Professor, in saying that every one of us at some point in our lives has come to this point. Sometimes these "familiar roads" that everyone takes can refer to events caused by peer pressure. The phrase "everyone's doing it, so it must be cool" comes to mind. In this sense, it is sometimes difficult to make your own path, even if other people aren't joining you. These "familiar roads" can symbolize the safe/easy way out of a situation rather than taking the risk and come out of the situation happier, more fulfilled and stronger.

Subject: re: That well-traveled road
Message no. 667 [Reply of: no. 641]
Author: Julie
Date: Tuesday, April 26, 2005 12:54pm

Wow, everyone has such a good analysis on this poem! It just goes to show you how differently this poem can mean to each person.

> This writer uses multiple conversation cues to build discussion.

Rene, I completely relate to the "What if" game you play! I do it constantly! Sometimes I question myself on even the littlest things that have happened in my past and would try to evaluate as to whether that would make me a much different person than I am today. I've learned from this game that, although it would be fun to see that alternative life, I am glad that I took the paths I took and made the choices I made. If I didn't, I wouldn't be as strong as I am today.

Brad, good observation on line 16, "I shall be telling this with a sigh".
Consider me the everlasting optimist, but I feel that he is saying it with a happy sigh. I feel that it is a sigh that expresses nostalgia and good memories.

Subject: re: That well-traveled road
Message no. 668 [Reply of: no. 641]
Author: Peter
Date: Tuesday, April 26, 2005 1:27pm

Perhaps I'm sappy, or perhaps I just love poetry and am just a fan of Frost, but I love this poem to pieces.

> This post is full of the kind of personal material that helps drive the boards and build a sense of community.

I'm definitely in the "It says a lot more than just how the story reads" group. Let me tell you why.

In our daily lives, we constantly make decisions. We decide toc omit to routines, to break routines, to communicate, to learn, to explore. One certain unforseeable days, we hit a splitin the path, and must make a life changing choice on which path to take. These are the decisions where one feels like they are losing control of their lives. As we play through the what-ifs of our choices, we seem to hit some sort of limit of how far in the future we can get with them. This isn't like deciding when to eat, we can clearly see a positive and a negative approach to such a decision.

Both paths look promising, beautiful, and will hold their own challenges.

Some of you know me quite well, with my work, school, and girlfriend, I feel like my life is just one mammoth fork in the road. When faced with such decisions, I feel this poem takes on a new meaning. It not only makes me feel like I'm not alone, but also gives some insight on the kind of man Frost was.

Back to the story...

The man takes the path less traveled... but why?

As someone had touched upon in the first post, decisions are made based on previous experiences, after all, it is only are own experiences that we are 100% sure of. I believe the story touches upon this by saying the paths were not taken before. The author has never been faced with such a decision and has never experienced these paths. He just knows what the "ground" looks like if someone has stepped on it, and how he perceives the path. Carefully analyzing the poem, the only qualities of these paths are preceptions from the author. In a funny twist, I question, did the author really take the "path" less traveled or did he only precieve the "path" to be less traveled?

What do we know about the author... that he's in the woods, walking on a path, that forks. There's a reason why he's in the "woods," that the reader doesn't know and in my opinion, anyone who walks through paths in the woods, comes back to the same location after thinking about it, and chooses a path is a person of adventure. My feeling for the reason behind the road less travelled is because it's an adventure, and has a sort of mysterious beauty about it. These kinds of adventures build and shape a person into who they are. I feel the text supports the "mysterious beauty." Look how Frost discuss the grass.

Closes with questions.

In addition to my other questions, what do you think the woods represent? Is the poem truly

about a man in the woods and we're all reading into this
WAY too much? Or is there something more to it?

Subject: Is it really the less popular path?

Message no. 688 [Reply of: no. 668]
Author: Scott Warnock
Date: Wednesday, April 27, 2005 3:40pm

Hey everyone,
You can definitely see this poem as encouraging you to take a risk and pick the less-traveled path in life: "I took the one less traveled by."

> I try to quickly summarize and act as a "generative guide."

However, several of you hint at the fact that really, they're the same. Peter says, "Carefully analyzing the poem, the only qualities of these paths are preceptions from the author. In a funny twist, I question, did the author really take the 'path' less traveled or did he only precieve the 'path' to be less traveled?"

Isn't there a lot of evidence in the poem that the paths are pretty much the same? Why does the speaker feel it's the path "less traveled" at the end then? Why do we like to feel that way?
Prof. Warnock

Subject: re: That well-traveled road

Message no. 679 [Reply of: no. 641]
Author: Karen
Date: Wednesday, April 27, 2005 12:59pm

"The Road Not Taken" by Robert Frost is one of the quintessential pieces one thinks of when they think of poetry. I've always thought the poem was not one of great complexity; I've always believed it is a poem

> Student finds a way to enter into the conversation . . .

that has a simple message. The message is to not necessarily go by what something looks like because outward appearance can be very deceiving. One road looks nice and grassy while the other doesn't look as well but in the end they "had worn them really about the same" (ln 10). The poem shows that we come to points in our lives where we have to make decisions. Whether they are difficult or an everyday choice, life is full of choices. As we mature we need to realize that the easy way out is not the best choice because most of the time it only seems to be the easy way out. This is why

Frost focuses on the road not taken. He makes the narrator decide to go against what everyone else is doing and understand that though the road is pretty and filled with trees and grass, it is not necessarily the road to be taken.

I believe Frost is also trying to advocate going with your own beliefs instead of going with the norm is important in life. It is another difficult choice that has to be made but one that will make you an individual and not just like everyone else. I can relate to this on a very simple level. When it came to deciding what college to attend I was left with two schools, Drexel and another big party school where most of my friends were going. Though I really wanted to attend the other school I chose to come to Drexel because I knew it would be better for me in the end. Now I'm already enrolled in a dual degree program and I'm focused on my future and what I want to do with my life as far as my education as well as my career. Unfortunately I can't say the same about my friends. Like the narrator of Frost's poem I made a choice because I looked ahead to my future. "I took the one less traveled by, /And that has made all the difference." (ln 19-20).

> ... then adds a new twist to the discussion.

Subject: re: That well-traveled road
Message no. 706 [Reply of: no. 641]
Author: Kathleen
Date: Thursday, April 28, 2005 1:37pm

I believe that the point that Frost is trying to get across is that in life everyone is faced with different decisions and many times you come across situations you need to make decisions for that no one else has had to make. It is hard to make decisions when you don't know what the outcomes will be. Frost says he "looked down one as far as I could" but he doesn't really know what is at the end of each road. While trying to make his decision he states that one looked to be "perhaps the better claim" but I think what he wants to get across is you shouldn't always make the decision that "looks" to be the right one because that tends to be the easy way out.

By concentrating on the road "less traveled by" he wants everyone to go against what everyone else would do and take a chance in life. Don't follow what everyone else does just because it's the easy way out or the safe way; take a chance just because you don't know the outcome

> This writer responds to my second prompt.

doesn't mean it's bad. Taking a chance in life and going against society can change your life greatly. I'm sure everyone can relate to this poem because everyone has to make decisions daily. I've read this poem many times and what I get out of it every time is to be different from everyone else and to make my own choices and don't just follow everyone else because it's easier.

Subject: re: That well-traveled road
Message no. 726 [Reply of: no. 641]
Author: Linda
Date: Thursday, April 28, 2005 11:28pm

Frost clearly says that the road less taveled is the better choice. I relate the two roads as the easy and the hard choices in life. We have all heard before that taking the easy way out is no way at all. If you take the hard road, while it might be very long and difficult, you will appreciate and enjoy the end result much more if you choose that one. That is the reason I conclude that Frost says he is happy he took the long road and does not regret his choice at all. The path that everyone took was the easy, shorter way, thus why so many people have taken it.

> Continues response to second prompt.

He reflects back upon his choice and does not regret it in the least because he is happier now that it is over and he is enjoying the results more so then those who had taken the easy way out. Perserverance and hard work pay off in the end, and I see this poem is a classic example of that.

Subject: re: That well-traveled road
Message no. 729 [Reply of: no. 641]
Author: Diane
Date: Thursday, April 28, 2005 11:57pm

Life is full of choices. Everyday people are faced with decisions that affect the future, whether it is short term or in the long run. In Frost's poem, the speaker is faced with a decision that will affect the rest of his life. **Frost focused on taking the road less traveled because going against the grain and popular choice takes courage.** I think the "roads" in Frost's poem can represent a wide variety of aspects in life. The roads are any choice made. The road less traveled could be not

> Continues response to second prompt.

going to college and starting a business, in a world
where it is difficult to find a job without a college education.

**It could also be seen as good vs. evil. It is easier to
fall into temptations and evil and take the easy path,
then to take the overgrown, tough but good path.**
Since the speaker took the harder path, he knows he will
have a good future. He worked for and earned whatever he
will receive. The speaker knows what is worked for means
more to a person then what they are just handed.

The speaker will grow and mature traveling the less
beaten path, and that is why he says "I doubted if I
should ever come back." **He knows that his state of mind
will be changed by his adventure.**

Subject: re: That well-traveled road
Message no. 759 [Reply of: no. 641]
Author: Katrina
Date: Saturday, April 30, 2005 2:56am

**You're right! We have all made that choice, more than
once in our lives. This poem exemplifies every day
decisions.** It is not over anaylized; it represents
every decision we make. When we make a decision, it's
obviously because we have more than
one choice or option, some more seri-
oius than others. Frost chose the road
not frequently taken. He wondered,
what would happen if he chose the other
road, which is normal. When we decide
to do something, or maybe not do some-
thing, there's always the curiosity, "what if...," and
he chose the road that most didn't. Frost chose the
road less traveled by. And sometimes, that's what we
have to do. You can't always listen to everyone, and do
what seems best or easiest at the time- take the road
less traveled by. It seems as though he took a chance,
and made a life for himself. You can't always be like
everyone else, or the way society wants you to be.
There are reasons we do what we do, and I feel as though
this poem is about following your instincts, and have
faith in yourself. As "corny" as it sounds, it's true.
**If you take the raod not taken, you are setting yourself
apart, maybe having to work harder, and doing things
differently, but that in itself is a learning experience.
Take the road not taken.**

> Again takes
> second prompt
> in a new
> direction.

Appendix D: Weblog Assignment

The weblog you will keep for this class will basically be an online response journal and commonplace book. A commonplace book, according to dictionary.com, is "a personal journal in which quotable passages, literary excerpts, and comments are written." You will use the blog to jot down useful and interesting words and passages and to respond to my specific questions about material we are discussing in the course. Feel free to make your weblog more elaborate, perhaps including graphics, a thematic structure, and/or additional entries.

Schedule and requirements
Starting in week two, I will supply you with prompts or questions that you will address on your weblog. If you delay the start of your weblog, you will quickly find yourself far behind and quite unhappy. Each entry must be

- clearly dated and
- contain the entry number.

Whenever appropriate the entries should also include links to other online material. You should write about 100 words per entry. The schedule for weblog entries will be posted in the Resources/Materials folder.

Evaluation
The whole endeavor will be evaluated based on the quality and depth of your responses, but I stress that sheer <u>diligence</u> will be rewarded here. The most damaging thing grade-wise is for you to skip entries. The weblog is worth <u>75 points</u>.

Publishing
I'm going to ask each of you to <u>publish</u> your weblog; that is, you'll at least share it with me and the other members of the class. However, you might want to think about a potentially broader <u>audience</u> for the weblog, and you may want friends and others to have access to it as well.

Hosts
I'm happy to talk to you about your blog, particularly some of the technical issues that are involved with getting a website up and rolling. Drexel makes it easy for you to start and host a rudimentary webpage. Start here: http://www.drexel.edu/irt/support/webits/ workshops.html. You may want to use one of the many commercial weblog hosts out there. For instance, you could start a blog on www. blogger.com within minutes. (Please note: "easy" does not mean

"instantaneous," but I think you'll find the process of getting Web space and starting your blog straightforward.)

Once you get your weblog up, I'll provide a place for all of us to post our URLs.

GLOSSARY

These terms appear in bold in their first mention in each chapter throughout the book.

asynchronous: not occurring at the same time; specifically in this book, communications software that does not require users to be present at the same time.

blended course: see *hybrid course.*

blog: website journal or diary on which a user writes messages ranging from the personal to the highly public.

chunking: combining smaller units of information into larger units.

CMS: course management system/software; usually a Web-based program to help teachers post materials, facilitate student conversations, and perform other class functions in online learning.

delicious: social bookmarking site that allows users to save, organize, and share favorite websites.

FAQ: frequently asked questions; a common area on many websites.

f2f: face-to-face or "normal" classes; also called *onsite* throughout the book.

FYW: first-year writing.

hybrid course: course that is taught half f2f and half online, although other proportions exist; in a hybrid course, you might meet your students for ninety minutes on Tuesday, and then on Thursday they would work in an online environment.

IM: instant messenger software, often used to facilitate chat conversations.

informal writing: writing that is low-stakes in a course; it might not be graded as rigorously as a formal assignment for aspects of mechanics, and it might be used as a tool to help students develop their thinking about a topic or idea.

learning object: a resource, often digital, that can be used and re-used to support learning.

learning outcome: a clear, specific goal for a course.

listserv: commonly used email mailing list software that enables users to send an email to a central email address and then have that message automatically emailed to everyone signed up for the list.

Luddite: one who opposes technical or technological change (based on a group of British workers who rioted in the early nineteenth century, destroying textile machinery in the belief that such machinery would supplant them).

macro: shortcut on a computer that allows you to execute a sequence of instructions quickly in abbreviated form, often by typing in a keyboard shorthand.

metadata: information accompanying a computer file that lists items such as author, date of creation, and document origin.

MOO: Multi-User Domain (MUD)–Object Oriented; an online community/virtual world in which users interact with each other via text; a MOO uses object-oriented methods of organizing its databases.

MP3: a common audio format; commonly used for transferring and playing digital music on audio devices.

MUD: Multi-User Dungeon; a virtual world in which the participants interact via text.

multimodal: communication using various media, including text, graphics, video, and audio.

OWcourse: online writing course.

PDA: lightweight, usually handheld digital device that serves a variety of functions, including communication tool, minicomputer, and planner.

PDF: Portable Document Format; common Web document format, created by Adobe Systems, that can be opened and read with Adobe Acrobat.

primary post: on a message board, a longish, substantive post.

project: any lengthy written essay, paper, assignment, or report; I use the term *project* because it captures the multimodal aspects of what students may be asked to do.

question sets: a group of questions on a quiz or examination from which a computer randomly selects a specific number of questions.

response: the feedback you provide and dialogue you open with students about their writing; this differs from straightforward grading.

reusable learning objects (RLO): electronic learning component that can be re-used in different environments.

rich text: common word processing document format.

SCORM: Sharable Content Object Reference Model; set of rules that a course management system uses to package learning materials in a way that allows them to be transferred.

screen capture: video or picture of a computer screen.

secondary post: on a message board, a shorter, response-type post.

synchronous: occurring at the same time; specifically in this book, communications software that requires users to be present at the same time, such as chat software.

thread: a particular topic of conversation on a message board.

Twitter: social networking/instant messenger software that allows users to tell subscribed friends what they are doing during the course of a day.

WAC: writing across the curriculum.

Web 2.0: term that refers to interactive Web tools and programs that allow people to collaborate, interact, and share information online.

Weekly Plan: organizational document that describes exactly what is due in a particular week in an online or hybrid writing course.

whiteboard: area of a computer screen on which users can write or draw; whiteboards are a component of teleconferencing and collaboration software.

WID: writing in the disciplines.

wiki: webpage or collection of pages that anyone can access and edit.

WORKS CITED

Addesso, Patricia. "Online Facilitation: Individual and Group Possibilities." White and Weight 112–23.

Albion, Peter R., and Peggy A. Ertmer. "Online Courses: Models and Strategies for Increasing Interaction." *AusWeb04: The Tenth Australian World Wide Web Conference.* Sea World Nara Resort, Australia. July 2004. *AusWeb04.* Web. 1 Feb. 2005.

Allen, I. Elaine, and Jeff Seaman. *Staying the Course: Online Education in the United States, 2008.* Needham: Sloan-C, 2008. *Sloan Consortium.* Web. 9 Jan. 2009.

Amrein, Audrey L., and David C. Berliner. "High-Stakes Testing, Uncertainty, and Student Learning." *Education Policy Analysis Archives* 10.18 (2002). Web. 30 Aug. 2008.

Anson, Chris M., ed. *The WAC Casebook: Scenes for Faculty Reflection and Program Development.* New York: Oxford UP, 2002. Print.

Arnoldy, Ben. "Students Sue Antiplagiarism Website for Rights to Their Homework." *Christian Science Monitor* 10 Apr. 2007: 1. Print.

Ashburn, Elizabeth A. "Attributes of Meaningful Learning Using Technology (MLT)." *Meaningful Learning Using Technology: What Educators Need to Know and Do.* Ed. Elizabeth A. Ashburn and Robert E. Floden. New York: Teachers College, 2006. 8–25. Print.

Austin M. Jill, and Linda D. Brown. "Internet Plagiarism: Developing Strategies to Curb Student Academic Dishonesty." *The Internet and Higher Education* 2.1 (1999): 21–33. Print.

Bakhtin, M. M. "Discourse in the Novel." *The Dialogic Imagination: Four Essays.* Ed. Michael Holquist. Trans. Caryl Emerson and Michael Holquist. Austin: U of Texas P, 1981. 259–422. Print. Univ. of Texas Press, Slavic Studies Ser. 1.

Barber, John F. "Effective Teaching in the Online Classroom: Thoughts and Recommendations." Harrington, Rickly, and Day 243–64.

Barker, Thomas T., and Fred O. Kemp. "Network Theory: A Postmodern Pedagogy for the Writing Classroom." *Computers and Community: Teaching Composition in the Twenty-First Century.* Ed. Carolyn Handa. Portsmouth: Boynton, 1990. 1–27. Print.

Bender, Tisha. *Discussion-Based Online Teaching to Enhance Student Learning: Theory Practice and Assessment.* Sterling: Stylus, 2003. Print.

Berkenkotter, Carol. "Writing and Problem Solving." Fulwiler and Young 33–44.

Bolter, J. David. *Writing Space: The Computer, Hypertext, and the History of Writing.* Hillsdale, N.J.: L. Erlbaum Associates, 1991. Print.

Bradley, Jean-Claude. Blog. *Useful Chemistry.* Web. 5 Feb. 2009.

Brandon, David P., and Andrea B. Hollingshead. "Collaborative Knowledge and Training in Online Groups." *Work Group Learning: Understanding, Improving, and Assessing How Groups Learn in Organizations.* Ed. Valerie I. Sessa and Manuel London. New York: Erlbaum, 2008. 285–313. Print.

Brannon, Lil, and C. H. Knoblauch. "On Students' Right to Their Own Texts: A Model of Teacher Response." *College Composition and Communication* 33.2 (1982): 157–66. Print.

Bray, Hiawatha. "Textbooks, Free and Illegal, Online." *Boston Globe* 18 July 2008. Web. 23 July 2008.

Breuch, Lee-Ann Kastman. *Virtual Peer Review: Teaching and Learning about Writing in Online Environments.* Albany: State U of New York P, 2004. Print.

Britton, James, Tony Burgess, Nancy Martin, Alex McLeod, and Harold Rosen. *The Development of Writing Abilities (11–18).* London: MacMillan, 1975. Print.

Brodkey, Linda. "Modernism and the Scene(s) of Writing." *College English* 49.4 (1987): 396–418. Print.

Bruffee, Kenneth A. "Collaborative Learning and the 'Conversations of Mankind.'" *College English* 46.7 (1984): 635–52. Print.

Byrd, Don, and Derek Owens. "Writing in the Hivemind." Taylor and Ward 47–58.

Calibrated Peer Review (CPA). Homepage. Web. 5 Feb. 2009.

Carbone, Nick. "Re: More on Loss of Traditional Literacy Online." Online posting. 21 Sept. 2008. *WPA-L Archives*. Web. 5 Feb. 2009.

Carico, Kathleen M., and Donna Logan. "A Generation in Cyberspace: Engaging Readers through Online Discussions." *Language Arts* 81.4 (2004): 293–302. Print.

Carr, Sarah. "Is Anyone Making Money on Distance Education?" *Chronicle of Higher Education* 16 Feb. 2001: A4. Print.

Cazden, Courtney B., and Sarah W. Beck. "Classroom Discourse." *Handbook of Discourse Processes*. Ed. Arthur C. Graesser, Morton Ann Gernsbacher, and Susan R. Goldman. Mahwah: Erlbaum, 2003. 165–97. Print.

Center for Social Media, School of Communication, American University. "Code of Best Practices in Fair Use for Media Literacy Education." Web. 5 Jan. 2009.

Cohen, Moshe, and Margaret Riel. "The Effect of Distant Audiences on Students' Writing." *American Educational Research Journal* 26.2 (1989): 143–59. Print.

Collison, George, Bonnie Elbaum, Sarah Haavind, and Robert Tinker. *Facilitating Online Learning: Effective Strategies for Moderators*. Madison: Atwood, 2000. Print.

Conceição, Simone C. O., ed. *Teaching Strategies in the Online Environment*. San Francisco: Jossey-Bass, 2007. Print.

CONFU: The Conference on Fair Use. Homepage. Web. 26 June 2008.

Conrad, Rita-Marie, and J. Ana Donaldson. *Engaging the Online Learner: Activities and Resources for Creative Instruction*. San Francisco: Jossey-Bass: 2004. Print.

Dawley, Lisa. *The Tools for Successful Online Teaching*. Hershey: Information Science, 2007. Print.

DeVoss, Dànielle, and Annette C. Rosati. "'It Wasn't Me, Was It?' Plagiarism and the Web." *Computers and Composition* 19.2 (2002): 191–203. Print.

Dewey, John. *Experience and Education*. The Kappa Delta Pi Lecture Series, [no. 10]. New York: Macmillan, 1938. Print.

Dibbell, Julian. *My Tiny Life: Crime and Passion in a Virtual World*. New York: Holt, 1998. Print.

Downs, Douglas, and Elizabeth Wardle. "Teaching about Writing, Righting Misconceptions: (Re)Envisioning 'First-Year Composition' as 'Introduction to Writing Studies.'" *College Composition and Communication* 58.4 (2007): 552–84. Print.

Drexel University, Department of English and Philosophy. "Online and Hybrid First-Year Writing Courses at Drexel University." Web. 12 Sept. 2008.

Drexel University, Information Resources and Technology. "Dragon-Drop." Web. 22 Dec. 2008.

Eberly, Mary B., Sarah E. Newton, and Robert A. Wiggins. "The Syllabus as a Tool for Student-centered Learning." *Journal of General Education* 50.1 (2001): 56–74. *Project Muse.* Web. 10 Sept. 2008.

Ede, Lisa, and Andrea Lunsford. "Audience Addressed/Audience Invoked: The Role of Audience in Composition Theory and Pedagogy." *College Composition and Communication* 35.2 (1984): 155–71. Print.

EduTools. "EduTools Course Management System Comparisons—Reborn." Web. 6 Jan. 2009.

Elbow, Peter. *Writing with Power: Techniques for Mastering the Writing Process.* New York: Oxford UP, 1981. Print.

Eldred, Janet M. "Pedagogy in the Computer-Networked Classroom." *Computers and Composition* 8.2 (1991): 47–61. Print.

Ericsson, Patricia Freitag, and Richard H. Haswell, eds. *Machine Scoring of Student Essays: Truth and Consequences.* Logan: Utah State UP, 2006. Print.

Faigley, Lester. *Fragments of Rationality: Postmodernity and the Subject of Composition.* Pittsburgh: U of Pittsburgh P, 1992. Print.

Fallows, James. "Making Haystacks, Finding Needles." *Atlantic Monthly* Nov. 2006: 140–43. Print.

Feenberg, Andrew. *Critical Theory of Technology.* New York: Oxford UP, 1991. Print.

———. "Distance Learning: Promise or Threat?" *United States Distance Learning Association (USDLA).* Web. 8 September 2008.

Fiske, Edward B., Sally D. Reed, and R. Craig Sautter. *Smart Schools, Smart Kids: Why Do Some Schools Work?* New York: Simon & Schuster, 1992. Print.

Fitzpatrick, Virginia. "An AV Aid to Teaching Writing." *English Journal* 57.3 (1968): 372–74. *JSTOR*. Web. 20 Feb. 2006.

Flores, Juan F. "The First Letter in Individual: An Alternative to Collective Online Discussion." *Teaching English in the Two-Year College* 33.4 (2006): 430–44. Print.

Flower, Linda, and John R. Hayes. "The Cognition of Discovery: Defining a Rhetorical Problem." *College Composition and Communication* 31.1 (1980): 21–32. Print.

Foster, Andrea L. "'Immersive Education' Submerges Students in Online Worlds Made for Learning." *Chronicle of Higher Education* 21 Dec. 2007. Web. 6 Feb. 2009.

Frechette, Julie. "Crossing the (Digital) Line." *Inside Higher Ed.* 16 May 2008. Web. 1 July 2008.

Freire, Paulo. *Pedagogy of the Oppressed.* New York: Continuum, 1992. Print.

Fullmer-Umari, Marilyn. "Getting Ready: The Syllabus and Other Online Indispensables." White and Weight 95–111.

Fulwiler, Toby, and Art Young, eds. *Language Connections: Writing and Reading across the Curriculum.* Urbana: NCTE, 1982. Print.

Gant, Camilla. "Scoring Asynchronous Discussions: An Exploratory Assessment Model." Distance Learning Administration (DLA) 2007 Conf. St. Simons Island, GA. 25 June 2007. Address.

Gardner, Howard. "The End of Literacy? Don't Stop Reading." *Washington Post* 17 Feb. 2008: B1. Print.

Gardner, Traci. "Dropbox: Your Online Filing Cabinet." Blog. *NCTE Inbox Blog.* NCTE, 16 Sept. 2008. Web. 6 Feb. 2009.

Garrison, D. Randy, and Norman D. Vaughan. *Blended Learning in Higher Education: Framework, Principles, and Guidelines.* San Francisco: Jossey-Bass, 2008. Print.

Gay, Pamela. "Improving Classroom Culture: Using Electronic Dialogue to Face Difference." Harrington, Rickly, and Day 147–58.

Gershenfeld, Neil. *When Things Start to Think.* New York: Holt, 1999. Print.

Giedion, Siegfried. *Mechanization Takes Command: A Contribution to Anonymous History.* 1948. New York: Norton, 1969. Print.

Gladwell, Malcolm. *Blink: The Power of Thinking Without Thinking.* New York: Little, Brown, and Company, 2005. Print.

Grego, Rhonda C., and Nancy S. Thompson. *Teaching/Writing in Thirdspaces: The Studio Approach.* Carbondale: Southern Illinois UP, 2008. Print.

Gudea, Sorin. *Expectations and Demands in Online Teaching: Practical Experiences.* Hershey: Information Science, 2008. Print.

Haas, Christina. *Writing Technology: Studies on the Materiality of Literacy.* Mahwah: Erlbaum, 1996. Print.

Haavind, Sarah. "Speaking in Voices: Effective Techniques for Keeping Web Discussions Running Smoothly." *Concord Consortium* Winter 1999. Web. 18 Sept. 2008.

Hanna, Donald E., Michelle Glowacki-Dudki, and Simone Conceicao-Runlee. *147 Practical Tips for Teaching Online Groups.* Madison, WI: Atwood, 2000. Print.

Hansen, Suzy. "Dear Plagiarists: You Get What You Pay For." *New York Times* 22 Aug. 2004. Web. 6 Feb. 2009.

Hanson, Sandra Sellers, and Leonard Vogt. "A Variation on Peer Critiquing: Peer Editing as the Integration of Language Skills." *A Sourcebook for Basic Writing Teachers.* Ed. Theresa Enos. New York: McGraw, 1987. 575–78. Print.

Harrington, Susanmarie, Rebecca Rickly, and Michael Day. "Introduction to the Online Writing Classroom: Supporting Teachers Who are Beginning to Use Technologies to Expand Notions of Literacy, Power, and Teaching." Harrington, Rickly, and Day 1–14.

———. eds. *The Online Writing Classroom.* Cresskill: Hampton, 2000. Print.

Haswell, Richard H. "Automatons and Automated Scoring: Drudges, Black Boxes, and Dei Ex Machina." Ericsson and Haswell 57–78.

———. "Documenting Improvement in College Writing: A Longitudinal Approach." *Written Communication* 17.3 (2000): 307–52. Print.

Hawisher, Gail E. "Electronic Meetings of the Minds: Research, Electronic Conferences, and Composition Studies." *Re-Imagining Computers and Composition: Teaching and Research in the Virtual Age.* Ed. Gail E. Hawisher and Paul LeBlanc. Portsmouth: Boynton, 1992. 81–101. Print.

Hawisher, Gail E., and Paul LeBlanc, eds. *Re-Imagining Computers and Composition: Teaching and Research in the Virtual Age.* Portsmouth, N.H.: Boynton/Cook, 1992. Print.

Hawisher, Gail E., and Cynthia L. Selfe. *Evolving Perspectives on Computers and Composition Studies: Questions for the 1990s.* Advances in Computers and Composition Studies. Urbana, IL: NCTE, 1991. Print.

———. *Passions, Pedagogies, and 21st Century Technologies.* Logan: Utah State University Press, 1999.

———. "The Rhetoric of Technology and the Electronic Writing Class." *College Composition and Communication* 42.1 (1991): 55–65. Print.

Hayes, Sandy. "Technology Tool Kit: Improving Writing: Online Bulletin Boards." *Voices from the Middle* 14.2 (2006): 71–73. Web. 8 July 2008.

Henderson, George, and Susan Smith Nash. *Excellence in College Teaching and Learning: Classroom and Online Instruction.* Springfield: Thomas, 2007. Print.

Henry, Jim. *Writing Workplace Cultures: An Archaeology of Professional Writing.* Carbondale: Southern Illinois UP, 2000. Print.

Hewett, Beth L., and Christa Ehmann. *Preparing Educators for Online Writing Instruction: Principles and Processes.* Urbana: NCTE, 2004. Print.

Hislop, Gregory W., and Heidi J. C. Ellis. "A Study of Faculty Effort in Online Teaching." *Internet and Higher Education* 7.1 (2004): 15–31. Print.

Hobbs, Renee, Peter Jaszi, and Pat Aufderheide. *The Cost of Copyright Confusion for Media Literacy.* The Center for Social Media at the School of Communication at American University. September 2007. Web. 19 December 2008.

Howard, Rebecca Moore. "Forget about Policing Plagiarism. Just Teach." *Chronicle of Higher Education* 16 Nov. 2001. *LexisNexis.* Web. 9 Sept. 2005.

———. "Sexuality, Textuality: The Cultural Work of Plagiarism." *College English* 62.4 (2000): 473–91. Print.

Hult, Christine A., and Ryan Richins. "The Rhetoric and Discourse of Instant Messaging." *Computers and Composition Online* Spring 2006. Web. 6 Feb. 2009.

"ISTE Unveils New Tech Standards for Teachers." *eSchool News* 11.8 (2008).Web. 18 Feb. 2009.

Johnson, E. Janet, and Karen Card. "The Effects of Instructor and Student Immediacy Behaviors in Writing Improvement and Course Satisfaction in a Web-based Undergraduate Course." *MountainRise, the International Journal of the Scholarship of Teaching and Learning*. Fall 2007. 1–21. Web. 11 Jan. 2009.

Kilby, Tim. "The Direction of Web-Based Training: A Practitioner's View." *Learning Organization* 8.5 (2001): 194–99. Print.

Kitzhaber, Albert R. *Themes, Theories, and Therapy: The Teaching of Writing in College.* New York: McGraw, 1963. Print.

Ko, Susan, and Steve Rossen. *Teaching Online: A Practical Guide.* 2nd ed. Boston: Houghton, 2004. Print.

Kolko, Beth E. "We Are Not Just (Electronic) Words: Learning the Literacies of Culture, Body, and Politics." Taylor and Ward 61–78.

Krucli, Thomas E. "Making Assessment Matter: Using the Computer to Create Interactive Feedback." *English Journal* 94.1 (2004): 47–52. *ProQuest.* Web. 15 Mar. 2006.

Kurzweil, Ray. *The Age of Spiritual Machines: When Computers Exceed Human Intelligence.* New York: Viking, 1999. Print.

Landow, George P. *Hypertext: The Convergence of Contemporary Critical Theory and Technology.* Baltimore: Johns Hopkins UP, 1992. Print.

Lanham, Richard A. *The Electronic Word: Democracy, Technology, and the Arts.* Chicago: U of Chicago P, 1993. Print.

Lavazzi, Tom. "Communication On(the)line." *South Atlantic Review* 66.1 (2001): 126–44. Print.

Lehman, Rosemary. "Learning Object Repositories." Conceição 57–66.

Lenhart, Amanda, Sousan Arafeh, Aaron Smith, and Alexandra Rankin Macgill. "Writing, Technology, and Teens." *Pew Internet and American Life Project.* Pew Research Center, 24 Apr. 2008. Web. 23 Aug. 2008.

Levine, S. Joseph. "Creating a Foundation for Learning Relationships." Levine, *Making* 17–24.

———. *Making Distance Education Work: Understanding Learning and Learners at a Distance*. Okemos, MI: LearnerAssociates.net, 2005. Print.

———. "The Online Discussion Board." Conceição 67–74.

Lewis, Chad. "Taming the Lions and Tigers and Bears." White and Weight 13–23.

MacWilliams, Bryon. "An Institution Is Shuttered for Its Western Ways." *Chronicle of Higher Education* 51.25 (25 Feb. 2005). Web. 20 March 2005.

Maguire, Loréal L. "Literature Review—Faculty Participation in Online Distance Education: Barriers and Motivators." *Online Journal of Distance Learning Administration* 8.1 (2005). Web. 5 Jan. 2009.

Maimon, Elaine P. "Talking to Strangers." *College Composition and Communication* 30.4 (1979): 364–69. Print.

Marcell, Michael. "Effectiveness of Regular Online Quizzing in Increasing Class Participation and Preparation." *International Journal for the Scholarship of Teaching and Learning* 2.1 (2008). Web. 9 July 2008.

Maricopa Center for Learning and Instruction, Maricopa Community Colleges. "Web Courseware Comparisons and Studies." 5 Feb. 2003. Web. 5 Jan. 2009.

Marsh, George E., II, Anna C. McFadden, and Barrie Jo Price. "Blended Instruction: Adapting Conventional Instruction for Large Classes." *Online Journal of Distance Learning Administration* 6.4 (2003). Web. 3 July 2008.

McKeachie, Wilbert J. *McKeachie's Teaching Tips: Strategies, Research, and Theory for College and University Teachers*. 11th ed. New York: Houghton, 2002. Print.

McLeod, Susan H. "Writing across the Curriculum: The Second Stage, and Beyond." *College Composition and Communication* 40.3 (1989): 337–43. Print.

McLuhan, Marshall. *Understanding Media: The Extensions of Man*. New York: McGraw, 1964. Print.

MERLOT: Multimedia Educational Resource for Learning and Online Teaching. Homepage. Web. 9 Feb. 2009.

Meyer, Katrina A. "Does Feedback Influence Student Postings To On-line Discussions?" *Journal of Educators Online* 4.1 (2007). Web. 24 May 2007.

Miller, Michael T., and Dann E. Husmann. "Strategies for Improving Instructional Delivery in Distance Education Programs." *Journal of Adult Education* 22.2 (1994): 23–29. Print.

Mount Holyoke College, Research and Instructional Support. "Course Management Systems." 16 May 2006. Web. 3 Dec. 2008.

Nagel, Dave. "Digital Divide? What Digital Divide?" *T.H.E. Journal* 23 June 2008. Web. 30 Dec. 2008.

National Council of Teachers of English. "The NCTE Definition of 21st Century Literacies." 15 Feb. 2008. Web. 4 March 2009.

Negroponte, Nicholas. *Being Digital.* New York: Vintage-Random, 1995. Print.

Nietzsche, Friedrich Wilhelm. *Twilight of the Idols, or How to Philosophize with a Hammer.* Trans. Duncan Large. London: Oxford UP, 1998. Print.

North, Stephen M. *The Making of Knowledge in Composition: Portrait of an Emerging Field.* Portsmouth: Boynton, 1987. Print.

Nystrand, Martin. "Learning to Write by Talking about Writing: A Summary of Research on Intensive Peer Review in Expository Writing Instruction at the University of Wisconsin-Madison." 1984. *ERIC.* Web. 9 Jan. 2009.

Ong, Walter J. *Orality and Literacy: The Technologizing of the Word.* London: Methuen, 1982. Print.

Palloff, Rena M., and Keith Pratt. *Collaborating Online: Learning Together in a Community.* New York: John Wiley & Sons, 2004.

———. *The Virtual Student: A Profile and Guide to Working with Online Learners.* San Francisco: Jossey-Bass, 2003.

Palmquist Mike. "A Brief History of Computer Support for Writing Centers and Writing-Across-the-Curriculum Programs." *Computers and Composition* 20.4 (2003): 395–413. *Science Direct.* Web. 6 May 2008.

Pollard, C. William. *The Soul of the Firm*. Grand Rapids: Zondervan, 2000. Print.

Pollard, Dave. "12 Tools That Will Soon Go the Way of Fax and CDs." Blog. *How to Save the World*. 5 Aug. 2008. Web. 28 Aug. 2008.

Purdy, James P. "Calling Off the Hounds: Technology and the Visibility of Plagiarism." *Pedagogy* 5.2 (2005): 275–96. Print.

Rich, Motoko. "Literacy Debate: Online, R U Really Reading?" *New York Times* 27 July 2008. Web. 29 July 2008.

Rife, Martine Courant. *The Importance of Understanding and Utilizing Fair Use in Educational Contexts: A Study on Media Literacy and Copyright Confusion*. 18 April 2008. Social Science Research Network. Web. 12 Dec. 2008.

Roszak, Theodore. *The Cult of Information: A Neo-Luddite Treatise on High-Tech, Artificial Intelligence, and the True Art of Thinking*. Berkeley: U of California P, 1994. Print.

Rushkoff, Douglas. *Playing the Future: What We Can Learn from Digital Kids*. New York: Riverhead, 1999. Print.

Russell, Arlene A. "Calibrated Peer Review™: A Writing and Critical-Thinking Instructional Tool." *Invention and Impact: Building Excellence in Undergraduate Science, Technology, Engineering and Mathematics (STEM) Education*. Washington: American Association for the Advancement of Science (AAAS), 2004. 67–71. Web. 3 Sept. 2008.

Salmon, Gilly. *E-Moderating: The Key to Teaching and Learning Online*. London: Kogan, 2000. Print.

Schank, Roger C. "Language and Memory." *Cognitive Science* 4.3 (1980): 243–84. Print.

Selfe, Cynthia L. *Technology and Literacy in the Twenty-First Century: The Importance of Paying Attention*. Carbondale: Southern Illinois UP, 1999. Print.

Selfe, Cynthia L., and Susan Hilligoss, eds. *Literacy and Computers: The Complications of Teaching and Learning with Technology*. New York: MLA, 1994. Print.

Simpson, Katherine P. "Collaboration and Critical Thinking in Online English Courses." *Teaching English in the Two-Year College* 33.4 (2006): 421–29. Print.

Slager, Melissa. "Can Technology Make Teens Better Writers?" *MSN Encarta*. 2008. Web. 5 Dec. 2008.

Sloan-C. Homepage. The Sloan Consortium. Web. 9 Feb. 2009.

Smith, Michael W., and Jeffrey D. Wilhelm. *"Reading Don't Fix No Chevys": Literacy in the Lives of Young Men*. Portsmouth: Heinemann, 2002. Print.

Smith, Robin M. *Conquering the Content: A Step-by-Step Guide to Online Course Design*. San Francisco: Jossey-Bass, 2008. Print.

Sommers, Nancy. "Responding to Student Writing." *College Composition and Communication* 33.2 (1982): 148–56. Print.

Spigelman, Candace. *Across Property Lines: Textual Ownership in Writing Groups*. Carbondale, IL: Southern Illinois UP, 2000. Print.

Stansbury, Meris. "Online Insight: Challenges Beat Cheerleading." *eCampus News* 8 May 2008. Web. 1 July 2008.

Stedman, Barbara. "Hooked on 'Tronics, or Creating a Happy Union of Computers and Pedagogies." Harrington, Rickly, and Day 19–28.

Stone, Brad, and Motoko Rich. "Turning Page, E-Books Start to Take Hold." *New York Times* 24 Dec. 2008: A1. Print.

Taylor, Todd, and Irene Ward, eds. *Literacy Theory in the Age of the Internet*. New York: Columbia UP, 1998. Print.

Tenner, Edward. *Why Things Bite Back: Technology and the Revenge of Unintended Consequences*. New York: Vintage-Random, 1997. Print.

Thompson, Brad. "If I Quiz Them, They Will Come." *Chronicle of Higher Education* 21 June 2002: B5. Print.

Thorne, Kaye. *Blended Learning: How to Integrate Online and Traditional Learning*. London: Kogan Page, 2003.

Thornton, Patricia, and Chris Houser. "Using Mobile Phones in Education." *Proceedings of the 2nd IEEE International Workshop on Wireless and Mobile Technologies in Education*. Ed. Jeremy Roschelle, et al. Los Alamitos: IEEE Computer Society, 2004. 3–10. Print.

Turkle, Sherry. *Life on the Screen: Identity in the Age of the Internet*. New York: Simon and Schuster, 1995.

Ugoretz, Joseph. "'Two Roads Diverged in a Wood': Productive Digression in Asynchronous Discussion." *Innovate* 1.3 (2005). Web. 28 Mar. 2007.

Upadhyay, Nitin. "M-Learning—A New Paradigm in Education." *International Journal of Instructional Technology and Distance Learning* 3.2 (2006): 27–34. Print.

Vavoula, Giasemi, et al. "Learning Bridges: A Role for Mobile Technologies in Education." *Educational Technology* 47.3 (2007): 33–36. Print.

Wahlstrom, Billie J. "Communication and Technology: Defining a Feminist Presence in Research and Practice." Selfe and Hilligoss 171–85.

Warnock, Scott. "And Then There Were Two: The Growing Pains of an Online Writing Course Faculty Training Initiative." Distance Learning Administration (DLA) 2007 Conf. St. Simons Island, GA. 26 June 2007. Address.

———. "'Awesome Job!'—Or Was It? The 'Many Eyes' of Asynchronous Writing Environments and the Implications on Plagiarism." *Plagiary* 1.12 (2006): 178–90. Print.

———. "Early Message Board Posters and Success in an Online Writing Class." Blog. *Online Writing Teacher*. 11 Apr. 2006. Web. 10 Feb. 2009.

———. "Quizzes Boost Comprehension, Confidence." *Teaching Professor* 8.3 (2004): 5. Print.

———. "Responding to Student Writing with Audio-Visual Feedback." *Writing and the iGeneration: Composition in the Computer-mediated Classroom*. Eds. Terry Carter and Maria A. Clayton. Southlake: Fountainhead Press, 2008. 201–27. Print.

Waypoint Outcomes. Homepage. Subjective Metrics. Web. 11 Feb. 2009.

Weller, Martin. "Assessment Issues on a Web-based Course." *Assessment & Evaluation in Higher Education* 27.2 (1 March 2002): 109–16. Print.

Western Cooperative for Educational Telecommunications. *No Significant Difference Phenomenon Website*. Web. 11 Feb. 2009.

White, Ken W., and Bob H. Weight, eds. *The Online Teaching Guide: A Handbook of Attitudes, Strategies, and Techniques for the Virtual Classroom*. Boston: Allyn & Bacon, 2000. Print.

Wiener, Norbert. *Cybernetics: Or, Control and Communication in the Animal and the Machine.* New York: Wiley, 1948. Print.

Williams, Sadie. "How Do I Know If They're Cheating? Teacher Strategies in an Information Age." *Curriculum Journal* 12.2 (2001): 225–39. Print.

Winner, Langdon. *The Whale and the Reactor: A Search for Limits in an Age of High Technology.* Chicago: U of Chicago P, 1986. Print.

Withrow, Frank B. *Literacy in the Digital Age: Reading, Writing, Viewing, and Computing.* Lanham: Scarecrow, 2004. Print.

Wolf, Patti. "Efficient and Effective Organization of an Online Class." Center for Teaching and Learning, University of Maryland University College. Web. 23 Aug. 2008.

Wood, Julie M. "A Marriage Waiting to Happen: Computers and Process Writing." *EdTech Leaders Online (ETLO).* Education Development Center, 2000. Web. 3 July 2008.

Wood, Nancy V. *Perspectives on Argument.* 5th ed. Upper Saddle River: Pearson-Prentice, 2007. Print.

Young, Jeffrey R. "Study Finds Hybrid Courses Just as Effective as Traditional Ones." *Chronicle of Higher Education* 16 Sept. 2008. Web. 18 Sept. 2008.

INDEX

AUTHOR

Scott Warnock is assistant professor of English and director of the Freshman Writing Program at Drexel University. He has coordinated the Drexel Department of English and Philosophy's initiative to offer online and hybrid composition courses. Warnock's research and teaching interests focus on uses of technology in writing instruction. He is also interested in writing assessment, writing in the professions, and how technology can facilitate better methods of responding to student work. He has spoken about teaching and technology issues and opportunities at numerous national conferences, and he has published his work in several book anthologies and venues such as the *Journal of Business and Technical Communication*, the *Journal of Technical Writing and Communication*, *Kairos*, *Plagiary*, *Learning Technology*, *The Teaching Professor*, and *Science Communication*. Warnock maintains a blog about online writing instruction called *Online Writing Teacher*. He is co-founder of Subjective Metrics, Inc., a company created to develop Waypoint writing assessment and peer review software. Warnock lives in a special place, the beautiful South Jersey community of Riverton, where he is surrounded by supportive neighbors, friends, and family. He spends his onsite life with Julianne, his wife of fourteen years, and three bright-eyed, energetic children: Elizabeth, 9; Nate, 7; and Zachary, 5.

This book was typeset in Sabon by Barbara Frazier.
The typeface used on the cover is Industria Solid.
The book was printed on 50-lb. Williamsburg Offset paper
by Versa Press, Inc.

DATE DUE

DEMCO